THE BOOK OF MOM:
What Parents Know by Heart

Tammy Bundy

ST. ANTHONY MESSENGER PRESS
Cincinnati, Ohio

Scripture citations are taken from the *New Revised Standard Version Bible,* copyright ©1989 by the Division of Christian Education of the National Council of Churches of Christ in the U.S.A. and used by permission.
Cover and book design by Mark Sullivan

Library of Congress Cataloging-in-Publication Data

Bundy, Tammy M., 1961-
  The book of mom : what parents know by heart / Tammy Bundy.
      p. cm.
  ISBN 0-86716-505-7 (pbk.)
  1. Motherhood—Religious aspects—Catholic Church. I. Title.
  BX2353.B86 2003
  248.8'431—dc21

                              2002155148

ISBN 0-86716-505-7
Copyright ©2003, Tammy Bundy
All rights reserved.
Published by St. Anthony Messenger Press
www.AmericanCatholic.org
Printed in the U.S.A.

To Megan, Katey, Ryan, and Evan . . .
. . . for teaching me so much.
I'm loving you.

Contents

Preface

"Don't look, Mommy."

The source I refer to as *The Book of Mom* which we mommies carry in our heads at all times, warns us of these words. Usually when we hear our children tell us not to look, they have, more often than not, done something with either a permanent marker or a pair of scissors.

But, since these words were spoken around Mother's Day, they somehow had a more innocent sound.

"Don't look, Mommy," my youngest daughter requested, while holding a shiny jewelry box from a Mother's Day display at a discount store a short while before the big day. Before I obediently walked away, I could see her combining her money with her older sister's.

Turning my attention to my six-year-old son, who had come with me for the sole purpose of spending his birthday money, I continued shopping. While we were searching for the perfect prize, my daughter found me again and seriously quizzed me, "Mommy, what do you want for Mother's Day?"

Again drawing upon *The Book of Mom* in my head, I replied as many moms before me have replied, "Oh, I don't need anything. I just want my children to be healthy and happy."

Completely dissatisfied with that vague reply, she continued, "No. What is it you really, really want?"

Remembering what she and her sister had been conferring over before, I simply stated, "Oh, you know, I really could use a jewelry box."

A mischievous smile came over her face as she walked away saying, "Don't look, Mommy!"

Later, with the birthday money finally spoken for, my son and I stood in line waiting to pay for his selections. He was holding two items, one of which was a bird figure on a stick intended for a garden display. He had picked this out because he is quite fond of his feathered friends. But while in line he grinned at the figure and asked, "Do you like this bird, Mommy?"

"It's great," I answered without much enthusiasm.

"No," he pressed further, "do you *really* like this bird?" Flipping through the pages of *The Book of Mom*, I finally translated what he was saying. "Oh, yes," I passionately responded. "I absolutely *love* that bird on a stick."

"Then I know what I am getting you for Mother's Day," he proudly announced. "Don't look, Mommy."

And lastly, there was my youngest child's present to me. As the baby of the family, his biggest concern was that he, personally, was not getting any presents at all on Mother's Day, and that just didn't seem fair. But he gave me my gift the day before, without even realizing it.

I was trying to get some writing done on my computer while he was amusing himself by climbing the viburnum tree next to my window. Every few minutes he would make the "Don't look, Mommy" request and disappear into the tree. Then he would appear again at my side bearing a blossom. "Here, Mommy," he would say with pride as he lay it on the computer.

Eight trips and just as many blossoms later, I finally realized what a task the whole procedure was for my little boy. Each blossom he had presented me with represented his climbing the tree, plucking a blossom, climbing down again and returning to bestow it upon me.

Finally giving him my undivided attention, I looked at the sweet smelling blossoms scattered on my computer and complimented, "Honey, this was so much work for you. Why did you do all this?"

Before he returned to the tree on his quest for more blossoms, he paused long enough to answer, "Because I'm loving you."

And watching a little bug scurry across my blossom-covered computer, I blinked back the tears as I thanked God for all my little treasures.

The Book of Mom in my head tells me days like this don't hang around for long.

I think I'd better look while I can.

And I invite you to look with me now. It's nothing new and complicated. In fact, it's pure and simple. I suspect you might even know it . . . by heart.

CHAPTER ONE:
The Happy Heart

A glad heart makes a cheerful countenance.
—Proverbs 15:13

THE WORKOUT

The season for sweating had begun.

I am not referring here to the weather, but rather to those of us who had eaten one too many Christmas cookies, two too many Valentine's candy boxes and heaven knows how many chocolate Easter eggs.

Yes, the pools would open soon and we would have to fit into our swimsuits again.

With this off-season thought somewhere in the back of my mind, I decided to plan ahead. Back in February, with a determination that is so unlike me, I joined the YMCA. I immediately took the workout orientation. And then with a culmination that is so like me, I went a sum total of one time.

Two months later, I decided I needed to get motivated. It was not that I felt I was in hideous shape. It was simply a desire to have all my body parts cease movement when I stopped moving. I was fed up with having my upper arm continue to passionately wave to someone, long after I had quit the action of waving. So I did that which one needs to do to get motivated. I bought expensive workout shoes.

One month after that, I finally felt inspired to sweat. As I was taking the price tag off those workout shoes, ready to search for the buff body I am sure lurks somewhere under the body of the woman who has had four babies, my oldest asked where I was going.

Answering that I was on a quest for fitness, she asked if I could, instead, stay home and exercise with her.

Now, I suspect the main reason we moms join health clubs is not just to get rid of our baby fat, but to have a place to go that is far away from our babies of all ages. Still, it was hard for me to turn down her request.

You see, my daughter, who had just turned twelve, was in what I call a low maintenance phase. Many warned me that it was a temporary lull in action before the teen years hit. But still, I couldn't deny that she just didn't need me as much anymore.

Bubble baths with Mom's help had long been replaced with solo showers. Requests for bedtime stories had been substituted with requests for a later bedtime. And learning how Mommy always makes a boo-boo all better was replaced by simply learning how not to cry.

Without a doubt, she was becoming more and more self-sufficient.

I believe it's called growing up.

I knew all along it was supposed to happen. I just hadn't expected it to happen so fast.

So, when my oldest child actually asked to spend time with her old mom instead of with one of her many young friends, I couldn't refuse.

And so it was that we were soon in our exercise studio, also known as my living room, with the rug pushed back. There I was trying to teach her Richard Simmons's *Sweatin' to the Oldies* as she attempted to instruct me on the finer points of Billy Blanks's *Tae-Bo Workout.*

That endeavor soon gave way to her version of "The Electric Slide" and my version of "The Hustle." If the truth were told, I'm sure we did more giggling than sweating, but somewhere along the way, the goal had changed.

For over an hour we jumped, danced and laughed together. And that word "together" had never seemed so important to me before.

I have no idea if our mother-daughter workout will ease the trauma associated with the jiggles of swimsuit season. I am not even sure one could call it cardiovascular.

But I know one thing for certain. It definitely was good for my heart.

LET'S DO LUNCH

One day my husband stopped by the house in the middle of a workday because he just happened to be in the neighborhood, having gone to lunch at an outstanding local restaurant. Accompanying him to this fine eating establishment were three of his female co-workers.

Now, as a stay-at-home mom, the phrase "let's do lunch" means nothing to me. The closest I had ever come to a "power lunch" was when the Happy Meal toy at McDonalds was a Power Ranger. Frankly, on most days, I am lucky if I am eating lunch while seated somewhere other than in my car.

But that was about to change.

Encouraged by that competitive gene that festers in all married souls, I decided, as my grandma would have said, "What's good for the goose, is good for the gander." Now it was my turn for a lunch date.

And so it was that I found myself in the car, on my way to lunch with two men. Okay, they weren't exactly men yet. But in about fifteen years, they will be considered men.

I marveled at the beautiful summer day as I observed my dates' reflections in my rearview mirror. Being the independent sort of males, they had both picked out something special to wear on this particular lunch date. One was dressed in a Pokemon shirt and a pair of Cincinnati Reds shorts. The other had picked out a purple turtleneck sweater, which added an interesting contrast to his yellow swim trunks.

I coyly smiled at my two dates as we pulled in to our restaurant of choice. I have to admit, my heart beat a little faster immediately upon seeing those golden arches.

The
Book
of
Mom

I knew my dates well enough that I could order for them. I did, however, have to ask them for their drink selections. But, being a woman of the new millennium, I felt compelled to offer them both a suggestion. Caffeine free, of course.

When our waitress had taken our orders, I was pleased to see that my dates were not the freeloading type. Each dug deep into his pockets and they presented me with a total of thirty-seven cents and one gum ball.

I have to confess, my head swelled as we took our seats and my two gentlemen flattered me by arguing over who got to sit next to me. Once this little dilemma was solved, we began our dining experience with me seated proudly in the middle.

Now, I do recall my husband mentioning that his lunch date at that restaurant involved award-winning desserts from a nationally recognized chef. But I'm sure he didn't mention anything about a free toy. Or a play yard.

As if that weren't enough to top off my dining experience, my two dates were so kind as to leave me more than half their food to finish for them as they went off to play on the beckoning slides.

But, like all good times, this date, too, had to end. Soon, it was time to be heading back to the car and home again. And this time, in the rearview mirror, I could see my two little boyfriends both start to nod off, eyes fluttering until finally they were blissfully sleeping with sweet little grins on their faces.

I guess I do know how to have a power lunch, after all.

ANGEL PIN

One Sunday afternoon, I was taking on the task of cleaning out my jewelry box. No, this does not mean I was separating my diamonds from my rubies in my velvet-lined cedar chest. It simply means I was trying to find a pair of earrings that actually matched somewhere in the cardboard box that rests in my sock drawer.

Sitting on the edge of my bed watching this not-too-fascinating event was my youngest daughter. As she watched, she managed to request every two minutes, "Can I have that?"

Finally finding a cheap gold-painted angel pin I had bought last year as one of a dozen, I knew I had a rare opportunity to appease her outstretched hand.

Now, this daughter of mine tends to be on the dramatic side of emotions. Life is wonderful. Life is horribly unfair. She screams with laughter. She screams with tears.

For this reason, she is somewhat anxious. She is, as the expression goes, afraid of her own shadow.

This is exactly why I knew the angel pin would be an ideal way to calm her fears as well as to shoo her out of the room at the same time.

Her deep brown eyes widened as I explained how the angel pins are thought to keep you safe. I told her they are believed to protect you.

She regarded the cheap gold-painted pin as a wonderful treasure. She promised with all her heart to take good care of it.

As she walked out of the room holding it in her hand as delicately as a fragile butterfly, I returned to untangling the necklaces in my own hand.

Later that night during our bedtime routine, my treasure-collecting daughter asked me an out-of-the-ordinary question.

"Mommy," she began, "when we die, does God make us little again and we start all over, or do we just die and that's it?" After a brief talk about heaven, spirits and enough reincarnation theories to exhaust even Shirley MacLaine, I came up with what I thought was an interesting scenario.

"Wouldn't it be funny," I offered, "if we took turns being the mommy? You know, this time, I'm the mommy and you're the child. But next time, you are the mommy and I will be your child."

"Awesome!" she exclaimed for just a moment. And then, interrupting herself as if to keep her words from being written in stone, she nervously added, "No, Mommy. I don't want to be the mommy. I want you to be the mommy. Every time. Okay? Promise me you will always be my mommy. Forever."

Before I could even answer her, she jumped up from her bed and raced over to her own jewelry box, returning with the same angel pin I had given her only hours earlier.

Pinning it on my tattered bathrobe, she instructed me, "I want you to wear this all the time. Every day. Okay, Mommy?"

And as I hugged her tightly, I agreed with her casting decision. For if there is ever another time that I am in this play called life, I want to be the mommy again.

The pay may not have earned me diamonds and rubies. But I do own a pin that is genuinely priceless.

What Parents Know by Heart

SWINGING

I am a swinger.

Yes indeed, I do enjoy swinging from time to time.

Sometimes I swing in the privacy of my own backyard. And sometimes I swing in public.

Of course, this type of swinging is not for the fainthearted. Or those with weak stomachs either.

Yes, I love to swing.

Granted, I am not referring here to a lifestyle, but rather to a recreational activity involving a swingset.

There is just something about swinging on a swing that has always soothed me.

The other day, my preschooler and I were at the park. And I never have been able to resist a beckoning swing. (This may be why my oldest daughter never likes having her soccer games at a place with a playground.)

Nevertheless, it was here that I soon found myself swinging side by side with my youngest. I have to marvel at how some things trigger memories in us so dramatically that we can see, hear, feel and taste the moment of the memory as if it were happening to us again.

I remember when I was a little girl and I would swing for hours. With the wind gently blowing my pigtails back and forth across my freckled cheeks, I would keep my motion going by pumping my little legs back and forth and back and forth. Then, with a giggle, I would glide with the wind. Somehow I felt as if I really were defying gravity. With every upswing, I almost did believe I could fly.

And when I got very brave, I would tip my head all the way back until my arms were outstretched completely and I would close my eyes, allowing the motion to totally tickle my tummy. I had learned early on that the only thing to do at a time like that was to hold on tight and enjoy the ride.

And so it was that I once again, all these years later, could find myself swinging side by side with my youngest child. And of course, after the motion was in full swing, I shut my eyes and leaned backwards, holding on tight.

Suddenly I was not a mommy with four kids. I was swinging. And you just can't have concerns and worries when you are swinging. The years of responsibility and decades of dependability were no more prevalent than the idea of stopping. I hadn't grown up at all. I was swinging.

And then somewhere in my moment of memory and motion, I heard a little voice say, "Can you push me again, Mommy? Really high like last time?"

So I forced myself to stop swinging and land with my two mommy feet firmly on the ground. I began once again to push my son in his swing, listening to his squeals of delight at the memory of motion we were, together, creating for him.

Watching him, I couldn't help but think of how fast the years have flown. The pigtailed little girl with the wind beneath her had grown up after all. And as she stood watching her youngest child, she realized how quickly time still continued to swing by. Soon there would be no more little ones providing an excuse to hang out around swingsets.

But the lessons she learned swinging taught her something valuable. Because now she knows what to do with this precious gift that is so aptly called the present.

Hang on tight. And enjoy the ride.

Shake Your Bon Bon

Does anyone know what a bon bon is?

Now, I looked it up in my handy-dandy dictionary and learned that a "bonbon" is a type of candy with something in the center, but in this particular case, I don't think that is quite it.

Let me back up for a minute, here. To understand this question, you need to understand something about my family. You see, my kids and I have this admittedly odd way of relieving tension. When the day gets a little too much on the tense side and I'm not sure what the next thing out of my mouth will be, don't be surprised if one of my kids or I will be heard saying, "I need a chance . . . to dance!" With this we run like crazy people into the room with the CD player and turn on a fast song and, together, we all dance like no one's watching.

And now, here is where the bonbon question comes in. Lately, our favorite song to get silly with is "Shake Your Bon Bon" by the Latin heartthrob, Ricky Martin. The words to this chorus involve the not very subtle and somewhat artistically challenged repetition of the command, "Shake your bon bon, shake your bon bon, shake your bon bon . . ." And so on and so forth. Now, at this point in my life, there are, indeed, a lot of my parts shaking while I dance. However, I still remain in the dark as to what exactly is my bon bon.

Nevertheless, this has become a fun, tension-relieving part of our day. The kids and I will be dancing and crazily cavorting while even the dog gets in on the action. He immediately joins in by barking and running around in circles. Granted, this could actually be a commentary on my dancing ability. But this dance fever is enjoyed by almost everyone in the house. Except of course, my middle school-aged daughter. She is too old to act goofy and too young to know you need to every now and then. Plus, she still has a hard time forgetting about the day she innocently walked in the door after school with a couple of her friends. My youngest and I had just decided it was a great "chance to dance" and had begun our exaggerated movements in the dance hall that is actually our living room. Now, whatever my bon bon is, it is approaching middle age and my adolescent doesn't care to ever see it shaking in the presence of her friends again.

In spite of my oldest daughter's reluctance to dance with me, or perhaps because of it, I will continue to dance with anyone who is willing to dance with me. I'm old enough to know that the music doesn't play on forever. And I'm smart enough to understand that there will, indeed, be a day when I may not be able to find my bon bon, let alone shake it.

So, until then, my oldest can draw the blinds, the dog can bark and whoever wants to join me can shake their bon bon. Whatever it may happen to be.

CHAPTER TWO:
The Listening Heart

Just as water reflects the face, so one
human heart reflects another.
—Proverbs 27:19

THE ROCK

It has been said that you can learn a lot about someone by going through his trash and seeing what he has chosen to throw away. I hold to the belief that the opposite is also true. I think you can learn much about someone by seeing what he believes is important enough to save.

Of course, in my case, that would be just about everything. Yes, I am a packrat.

I had to confront this reality the other day when a sock drawer in my bedroom would not close. It was then I realized that drawer contained everything but socks.

And so, in my orderly way of cleaning, I dumped all the contents of that drawer on the floor. I was amazed at what the drawer had held. Thus began my unexpected trip down memory lane.

Some of my drawer discoveries were sweet. I found little notes each of my kids had written displaying various stages of their penmanship. I discovered photos long believed to have been lost. I even found a few baby teeth that the tooth fairy must have dropped in my drawer on her way out the window.

Some findings were simply ridiculous. There were tags off old outfits, receipts from groceries purchased four years earlier, and stale sticks of gum.

Still, some discoveries reminded me I was getting older. I actually found a crumpled piece of paper with an autograph of a then-young band that I had met after they performed at a disco. The band's name was Air Supply, and if you don't remember the group, you will at least understand by the word *disco* that the band, the paper and the person who saved it aren't getting any younger.

Then I saw my rock. It was the simplest thing, and yet it made me smile with this overwhelming sense of nostalgia. It was a polished rock that I remember getting from a friend of my parents. This man had a little business polishing rocks and selling them as jewelry. His name has escaped me after all these years, but the feeling I had when he showed me this beautiful rock and told me I could keep it, will never leave.

The rock itself had a varied texture of things I was supposed to have learned in Geology 101 but never did. All I know is that there was a river of something in my rock that I swore was made of diamonds. And it was mine and I was so proud of it.

Now, I was not born a coal miner's daughter. I did not want for too much while growing up. I had enough, but thankfully, not too much.

And as this hand of a woman touched the rock that had so touched the heart of a child, I still felt the emotion of holding a treasure. It was then that I began to wonder what it would be that my own kids would store in their sock drawers of life that would elicit such memories for them some thirty years from today.

Would they tear up upon finding their long lost Pokeman cards? Or is it Harry Potter now?

Would they feel that pure joy when they finally hold their Gameboy in their hands after so many years?

Perhaps it will be one of their hundred Beanie Babies that will make them turn misty upon rediscovery.

I know for a fact that my kids treasure everything they ever get. For about a week. And then they are ready to treasure something new.

In trying to give our kids everything, have we forgotten to give them something important? Have we truly given them the ability to appreciate and not just accumulate?

As I turn my attention back to the treasured memory in my hand, I can only hope I am doing enough to give to my children the gift of a foundation that is solid.

As a rock.

What

Parents

Know

by

Heart

MOMMY FISH

The other day, my little boy discovered something fishy. He learned a certain law of nature and it upset him.

It all started out innocently enough.

We were watching a television show aimed at kids. At one point in the show, it was discovered that a mother fish had had baby fish. There must have been thirty new little fish in the tank.

Then on the show it was mentioned that they needed to separate the mother fish from the babies for the protection of the new little fish.

My son couldn't wait for the televised explanation of this.

"Why do they have to take the babies away from the mommy?" my second grader asked about this seemingly unnatural action.

Calling upon my knowledge of aquatic life, which basically consists of the phrase, "One fish, two fish, red fish, blue fish," I managed to retrieve a piece of information from my ever-dwindling memory banks.

"Sometimes a mommy fish, if left in the same tank with her babies, will actually eat them."

While I was pleased with my explanation, my son looked aghast at the newfound knowledge, "That's disgusting!" he managed to comment. "Why would the mommy kill her own babies?" he demanded to know.

Realizing I would have to go deeper than Dr. Seuss for this one, I took a deep breath. "It's just something in nature that makes that happen. I really can't explain it."

The deep look in his eyes told me my vague answer had not satiated his quest for nautical knowledge.

He continued, "Do any other animals do that?"

I stammered out another obscure answer, "I think some other fish eat their young . . . maybe some insects . . . maybe some other animals. . . . I'm not completely sure."

Suddenly I wished I had taken better notes in biology class.

"What about dogs?" my little investigator continued, looking at his own pet, concerned for his safety. I assured him that his puppy was safe. I then made a blanket statement, saying that the larger animals usually take good care of their babies, not kill them.

Then we had to go through a list of all the animals in the zoo, as I assured him that motherly love was not an endangered species.

"What about people?" came the inevitable question.

I finally promised him then that the natural instinct of human mommies is to love their babies, care for them, feed them and tickle them. As I said that last part, I began to tickle my very inquisitive son to get him to smile again after such serious talk. When the giggles had subsided, I changed the channel.

Unfortunately, what was on the next channel was the scariest nature show of all. It was the news.

The lead story was about the approval of the abortion pill RU-486 for use in the United States.

"What does that mean?" my curious son asked immediately.

Remembering the promise I had just made on behalf of the law of human nature, I swiftly changed both the subject and the channel.

I knew, without a doubt, that announcement would simply be too bitter a pill to swallow.

Pilgrim's Pause

The only time I had ever thought of the word *pilgrim* was at Thanksgiving.

So when I was asked if I would like to be a pilgrim during my church's summer pilgrimage, I wasn't certain about what to expect. But I was curious.

I looked up the word *pilgrimage* in my dictionary. It said the word meant, "any long journey or search." With this in mind, I realized I would most likely not be expected to don a Puritan apron and cook a turkey.

And so I signed up for my very first pilgrimage.

It was not long before the whining and crying about my leaving began. But my husband soon got over it.

If the truth be told, he actually supported me in my weekend retreat. Four days spent in the company of soul-searching adults sounded like good medicine for the morale of any mom. Plus, he couldn't complain too much because he, himself, was planning to go the next weekend on a retreat to Cooperstown to, I believe, search for the true meaning of baseball.

So, with only a few expected complaints from my four kids about my journey, I began my weekend pilgrimage. And it was, indeed, a search and discovery time for me.

More and more we hear the world tell us we have to take care of ourselves. Advice telling us not to lose track of who we are fills every television channel, magazine and self-help book. But we moms seldom have the time to even watch TV or read. We are too busy wearing the mommy hat.

Now, I love my mommy hat. And I love my hats that metaphorically make me into a wife, a daughter, a writer and a friend.

But if we forget to take time to really get inside the head that each of those hats sits upon, we soon lose who we are in the first place.

Airlines are truly onto something when they give us advice on the oxygen masks that drop down from the ceiling in case of an air emergency. They advise us to first put the mask on ourselves, and only after having done that, put the mask on those who may be in need of our assistance. So many times in our lives, we get so caught up in trying to help everyone around us that we literally do forget to breathe.

For this reason, I was glad I took the opportunity to have a weekend away from those who need me the most, enabling me to focus on the woman who happens to be a mommy, instead of always focusing on the mommy who happens to be a woman.

The weekend was full of time to pray, think, feel and, yes, breathe.

By taking off my mommy hat, I was able to fill up my mommy heart.

When the weekend was over, this pilgrim put her mommy hat back on with pleasure. I had, indeed, had a pilgrimage—a journey or search—discovering one more time who was under all those hats I wear everyday.

And for this pilgrim, that is plenty enough reason for thanksgiving.

About Time

I knew it was about time.

Each year during the mornings when I am waking my kids up for school and the moon still appears to be shining in the night sky, I realize it is just about time for daylight savings time.

I always love the one in the fall. That "falling back" idea of actually getting an extra hour of sleep is so inviting to me. Gleefully, I flit around the house before going to bed, changing the hour hands on all our clocks, as if I were the self-appointed daylight savings fairy. I knowingly stay up later than usual, because I will, indeed, be able to sleep in an extra hour in the morning.

Of course, that was assuming someone told the kids about the whole "falling back" thing. Reality went something like this:

6:15 A.M.: My youngest finds his way into my bed yawning his question, "Mommy, is it morning, yet?" Assuring him it was not yet morning bought me a little more sleep (emphasis on the word *little*).

6:30 A.M.: Little one gets suspicious. "Mommy, are you sure it's not morning? I can see the light outside." I tried explaining that we changed the clocks last night, but he insisted they looked the same to him.

6:45 A.M.: When I had just managed to get my youngest to stop lifting the blinds, my other son makes his appearance by my bed with the question, "How much longer until Trick or Treat?"

Of course those magic words meant the end of any pretense of relaxation when the younger one was reminded of the night's coming events. We might as well get up.

I guess it was about time.

I think so much of my day is about time. I used to be quite good at getting somewhere actually on time. But that was before I did something that made it physically impossible for me to arrive at a certain destination at an appointed time. I had kids. I think it goes back to my first pregnancy test. I was late then, and I've been late ever since.

For this reason, I am guilty of the "I'm in a hurry and therefore, you must hurry" school of thought. On more days than I care to admit, I catch myself barking at my children to move more quickly simply because I had not allowed enough time to get somewhere.

Like the other day.

I had a few errands to run before I needed to get home in time to do a few more errands before my oldest three got home from school. I dashed off to the store with my youngest in tow. As was to be expected, I was frantically moving at a somewhat hyper pace to make up for my own tardiness. Of course, my son did what all little ones do two minutes before you get to where you are going. He fell asleep in the car.

Knowing that if I woke him up, I would have a cranky boy on my hands (as well as shoulders), I decided to let him sleep for just a little while longer. I turned off the car, only to hear the peaceful rhythm of his gentle breathing. This tranquil world soon beckoned me to come closer. I crawled into the backseat, sitting beside him, just watching him breathe. I'm not sure when it happened, but I soon realized that my own frenzied breath had begun to slow down to keep pace with his. So, there I sat for the longest time, doing nothing but watching my baby do nothing. But, somehow, it was really something. For while I was gazing at the face of my son, I was actually facing the reality of how quickly I am rushing past this precious breath of time called life.

I think I learned something that day.

You could say it was about time.

Truly, Madly, Deeply

One day I had a revelation.

It may mean nothing to anyone else, but to me it was huge.

I realized my youngest child was now the oldest "youngest child" I have ever had.

Now, after nearly twelve years of having a baby, on average, every three years, realizing your youngest is over three and there is no one on the horizon to take this title away from him, is big news.

I cannot tell a lie and pretend I was not happy with this milestone.

That is not to say I was rushing him to grow up too fast. My phone call to the Ohio State University about pre-admitting him for the year 2013 was simply a fact-finding mission.

But I have to admit, I did come close to hyperventilating when I picked up his pre-school registration form.

It's not that I didn't enjoy the time I got to spend with him while the other three were in school all day. I truthfully felt I was actually getting to know him better. It was just that I was looking forward to the day when I could spend time with myself and actually get to know "me" better.

No sooner did I allow myself to have that thought than something happened to help me refocus.

It was one of those innocent shopping excursions. I only needed a couple of things at the mall, so I figured I could run in and out in no time.

Of course, I had forgotten I was taking a three-year-old shopper along for the ride.

We adults have programmed ourselves to get from point A to point C without even looking at point B.

A child has yet to learn our "rushing through" way of life. Not only does he want to stop and look at point B, but he also has to touch it, admire it and try it out.

And these two shopping philosophies are destined to collide.

This was my frantic frame of mind as I was returning from my intended quick dash to the mall.

Trying to relax in the car, I gave in to my one bad habit. (Okay, if you were to ask my husband, he might be able to come up with more than one.) But my bad habit that I admit to is I tend to burst into song without even realizing I am singing. Now, this may not be too bad in a secluded car, but my oldest child refuses to go to the supermarket with me anymore due to this tendency.

This time I didn't even realize I had been singing until my little boy asked me a confusing question.

"*Me*, Mommy?" he asked.

Totally baffled, I stopped singing long enough to ask him what he had said.

"*Me*, Mommy?" he repeated, more excited this time.

And then I realized what he meant. The song on the radio I had been singing was by a group named Savage Garden and it was called "Truly, Madly, Deeply." I had just sung the lyrics:

> *I want to stand with you on a mountain*
>
> *I want to bathe with you in the sea.*

My son asked for the last time with more clarity, "Do you want to stand with me on a mountain, Mommy? Me?"

There was such flattered excitement in his three-year-old voice,

I had no choice but to answer, "Yes, you. I want to stand with you on a mountain."

"Thank you, Mommy!" he exclaimed and beamed as he listened to the rest of the song.

And I couldn't help smiling at his reflection in my rearview mirror as I watched his fulfillment in my acceptance.

Then it happened.

The last line of the song pierced straight through my heart as I listened as a guilty mom who had been dreaming of an easier tomorrow.

> *I want to live like this forever*
> *Until the sky falls down on me.*

Suddenly, I understood. This was all so temporary. We were *not* going to live like this forever.

And seeing my little one's adorable head bobbling to the music, still tickled by me wanting to stand with him on that mountain, made tears fill my eyes.

I guess I sometimes fail to realize I don't have to wait until my kids are older to discover who I really am. For I know I can always see my true identity simply by looking at my reflection shining back at me from the eyes of my children. And on those days when my vision is clouded with self-pity, I pray I will remember these really are the best of times.

"Truly, Madly, Deeply."

CHAPTER THREE:
The Patient Heart

Love is patient; love is kind; love is not
envious or boastful . . .
—1 Corinthians 13:4

HERO IN THE HOUSE

Romance novels.

I find that I have to admit I do enjoy a good romance novel every now and then.

As a former English teacher, I am sure many would assume that on any given moment when I might have a chance to indulge in the literary world, it would be by curling up with Shakespeare or Tolstoy. But the truth is, I find it hard to resist a cover depicting a heroine with a heaving bosom and a hero without a shirt.

I was thinking about the shirtless heroes of these books the other day when my daughter asked an out-of-the-blue question. "Mommy, is Daddy your hero?"

Stifling my laughter, I assured her he was my hero, even

though he *is* partial to shirts.

Then I had to smile at the memory my mind immediately conjured up displaying for me a moment of my husband's heroism. Now, this has nothing to do with pirates or castles, but to me, it was nothing short of heroic.

A while back, my husband had a routine with our two youngest. Each night, when he would say goodnight, they would ask him to "fly." This involved the boys being lifted up and circling their bedroom until they would plop into their waiting beds. This flight pattern would always result in more squeals than slumber, but the pilot and young airplanes delighted in it.

But that is not the hero part.

A few months earlier, after years of hodgepodge furniture, my husband and I took the decorative plunge and decided to buy a roomful of furniture that looked like it actually belonged together. This was a big step for us and the resulting room left us with a place we could point to with pride.

Of course, then we had to let the children back into the room.

Before the bill for the furniture had even arrived, our youngest, then two years old, decided the existing light green fabric on the ottoman needed a change of color and took the task on himself, armed with a ballpoint pen.

My husband was the first to discover the artwork and the guilty tears of the toddler gave him away.

Daddy was firm but fair in his discipline to our budding Picasso.

But that is not the hero part.

A half-hour later, it was bedtime. The would-be artist was tucked into his toddler bed, his big eyes trying hard not to cry again. "Fly, Daddy?" he asked his father about their nightly ritual.

"Daddy's not going to fly tonight," my husband carefully explained. "Daddy is still very upset about your coloring on our new furniture. So no 'fly' tonight, okay?"

Our youngest child bit his trembling lip as he bravely accepted his punishment. He nodded his head and answered, his voice cracking, "Okay, Daddy."

And at that point, my hero looked at our convicted colorer and smiled. "But then again, you *are* only two years old, aren't you?"

As the aviary artist flew into bed that night, I saw through my own tears what a hero was to me.

Sure, his shirt was on and my bosom wasn't heaving.

But then, I didn't need a hero to defend my land or my honor. I just needed a hero who understood that furniture might be expensive, but the most valuable things in our house walk, talk and, yes, color.

What
Parents
Know
by
Heart

THE ANGST OF ADOLESCENCE

Not too long ago, there was a stranger walking around my house. Yet the dog wasn't barking. He seemed to recognize this person. But I didn't.

This stranger looked like an older version of my firstborn. She would wear my daughter's clothes (and a good deal of mine as well). You see, this stranger was my daughter. She was twelve . . . going on twenty-one.

There is nothing stranger than adolescence.

I had come face to face with this sobering fact a while back. And this fact became even more strange than fiction when I would remember that my oldest used to be such an easy child. I have a theory, based on nothing scientific at all, which holds to the belief that all firstborn children are fairly easy-going kids. I think this is God's way of ensuring the population keeps growing. So, he gives us a really easy firstborn and we get so overly confident in our self-assured parenting techniques that we go and do something silly. We keep having children. This is further proof, for me, that God has a sense of humor.

And then the firstborn hits adolescence. I'm still searching for the humor in that.

All at once, my happy and carefree child who used to swing in the backyard would spend all her free time on the phone. And the only thing swinging was her mood.

One day she asked that I buy her something. Now, I will try to say this without necessitating her having to go into the witness relocation program. She wanted me to buy her . . . new undergarments. While shopping for these undergarments, I pulled out a nice-looking sample and held it up for her inspection, asking the question, "What do you think of this one?" My daughter looked at what I was holding and then looked at me with an expression of pure horror. She seemed to be waiting for the other two hundred shoppers in the store to turn around simultaneously from their various departments and see what this girl's mother had just pulled out for her. And then she did what a preteen does best. She rolled her eyes and walked away.

Could this have been the same girl who at the age of three used to flash her Little Mermaid underwear to anyone who would notice?

The stranger was definitely in the house.

And nothing was stranger than a certain weekend. Returning rather late from her first boy-girl party, my daughter walked in the door. My sincere requests for details were met with yawns and one-word responses. Then, suddenly, she looked very awake. I suspected I was about to get the full report I had been waiting for. "I *have* to call Madeline," she exclaimed as she raced to the phone.

I explained in my coolest mom's voice that it was, indeed, too late to phone a friend, but maybe she could share with me what she wanted to share with her friend.

I hadn't realized how far she actually could roll those brown eyes of hers.

Now, as a preteen, she still could have her familiar moments when I would actually stop suspecting a scene from *Invasion of the Body Snatchers* had occurred at my house. Nevertheless, I have to admit the changes, both physical and emotional, are enough to take my breath away.

After my oldest had gone to bed that night, I lay in my own bed,

*What
Parents
Know
by
Heart*

thinking of the familiar stranger in the other room.

At that very moment, my youngest appeared at the side of my bed. "Mommy, I'm scared. Can I sleep with you for a little while?"

A minute later, he was cuddled next to me, but only after I made him promise me two things: No kicking in his sleep.

And no growing up.

The

Book

of

Mom

THE ELEVATOR

We walked into the elevator at the same time.

On any other occasion, I might not have noticed. But this was an elevator at Children's Hospital. Everyone was there for a reason that remains a respectful mystery to those passing by.

Now, my husband and I were on this elevator with our middle daughter hoping to get some answers to why she suffers from headaches. We had passed hallways marked with names of medical conditions and procedures that I could not even pronounce, let alone understand. We had just come from the only one I did understand: radiology.

As we walked into the elevator, I noticed another mother with her child, holding on to her son's shoulders in the same protective manner in which I was clutching my daughter's shoulders. I had no idea what had brought them to the hospital, or what news they were taking home with them. Likewise, she had no idea what our story was.

She did not know that just a few minutes earlier, my daughter lay in a futuristic tunnel device staring at Little Mermaid stickers while the dye which was placed in the IV in her arm made the inside of her head glow on the monitor. And the other mother had no idea that while I was holding onto my husband as we watched, I strangely remembered another time almost ten years earlier. I flashed back to the day when my husband was again at my side and we first got a look at our as-yet-unborn daughter through another futuristic device called an ultrasound. Upon seeing my baby for the first time, I felt for certain I could not possibly love her more than at that very moment. But standing there, in Children's Hospital as she lay strapped to the stretcher-like gurney, I understood that the love I knew then could not even come close to the passion of parenting I was experiencing now.

In the elevator I wondered what kinds of tests the other mother had to watch her child endure. Were they, too, at the beginning of their journey, or was it almost over? But, somehow, it did not seem like the place to start chatting about our individual days. And as we both got off the elevator, my eyes linked but for a moment with the other mother's. We politely smiled and then quickly averted our gazes before either of us learned more than we had wanted to know about the other. Nothing was said, but everything was understood.

Now, she never knew that the next day, we got good news on a very treatable course of action for my daughter. The other mother would not know that I cried with thanksgiving after the phone call that I feared had the potential to change all our lives.

And I will never know whether she received a phone call that would bring her either tears of joy or sorrow.

All I would ever know about the other mother was that we had simply shared an elevator at an incredibly vulnerable time, when neither of us knew exactly where the ride would end.

The

Book

of

Mom

Paper Predicament

Some people think of grade cards and graduations as the perfect symbols of the end of the school year, but for me it is something different.

It is my cupboard.

For me, nothing symbolizes the culmination of a year on the journey of academic pursuit more than one particular cupboard in my house. It is here that I store all of those take-home papers, tests, artwork, notes and other varied treasures of the past school year. And as I survey the mammoth mound of papers depicting the ardent strides my children have made during the last nine months, one single thought fills my mind: What on earth am I going to do with all this stuff?

I believe there is a law written somewhere in the parent handbook that states it is illegal to throw away anything your child hands to you with pride. No matter if the child spent approximately thirty seconds scribbling on a napkin with a red marker, creating something that is not even discernable to the naked eye, the parent must do the mandatory praise and promise to keep that napkin forever, or maybe even longer.

And that is why I have the aforementioned cupboard. I seriously ascertain that I currently have enough schoolwork stored in this cupboard to wallpaper every room in my house with enough left over to line all our dresser drawers.

But the cupboard is not where the important papers go first. Before landing in that final resting place, the artwork or an exceptional test will most often take a journey from the backpack to the family billboard that is also known as my refrigerator. This gives the treasures a place to stay until they turn yellow or fall off and are chewed to unrecognizable proportions by the dog. An added bonus to placing them on the refrigerator is that this encourages the kids to practice math skills as they suspiciously add up the number of their displayed works compared to the displayed works of their siblings.

Once the prized paperwork has hung on the refrigerator long enough to start to curve into a scroll, it is time to replace it with a new treasure and retire the original work to the cupboard.

But I must confess. I have broken the law of that parental handbook. Sometimes, in a moment of weakness, like when the cupboard will no longer close, I have been known to break down. This is the time that I first throw caution to the wind and then throw an innocent paper into the trash.

And I always get caught.

Now, I know better than to lay the unwanted paper in the trash can in plain sight. I have had my mommy badge for a lot longer than that. For that reason, I will meticulously fold what I feel is a paper whose time has come and bury it deep in the waste receptacle. And of course, that is always the time one of my kids will uncharacteristically volunteer to help carry out the trash, leaving them to discover my transgression somewhere between the kitchen and the curb.

And as they stand in the doorway with a six-month-old ketchup-stained spelling test in their hand and a look of betrayal in their eyes, I realize there is only one thing I can possibly say to save this situation.

"Daddy did it."

THE SOCK SYNDROME

I once heard it said that childhood is a time when little ones are taking mental pictures that they will forever hang in the museum of their mind. Wouldn't it be wonderful if all the pictures our kids were hanging up were only along the lines of Norman Rockwell scenes?

Unfortunately, all of family life is not a Kodak moment.

How many times do we parents hear words coming out of our own mouths and into our kids' ears, while we wonder who is talking to our children in that manner?

I confess—this happened to me not too long ago.

At my house we have a sad situation that I refer to as "the sock syndrome." While I have never seen a telethon or organized fundraiser for this syndrome, I suspect it rears its ugly little head at other homes as well. The primary, and for that matter only, symptom of this syndrome is that there is never a matching pair of socks in a home for more than one week at a time. In the last year alone I have purchased roughly one thousand pairs of socks and somehow, when the kids start to grab them on their way out the door, they can never find two matching mates.

What
Parents
Know
by
Heart

For this reason I am often spending more time than I care to admit hopelessly trying to find some semblance of a match of socks on the nights before school.

This is where I had just come from on that particular night. After twenty minutes of sorting through piles of white socks with red tips, white socks with blue tips, white socks with no tips, I finally found a pair of socks that looked like they might actually belong together. Then, that wonders might never cease, I found another.

Two pairs of matching socks at my house are literally unheard of. I proudly walked upstairs with my prized possessions and laid the two matches down on the floor, while I went to get a towel for my seven-year-old who was just finishing his bath. As I turned around, my youngest child picked up the two precious pairs of socks and threw them at his brother who was still sitting in the tub as he yelled to him, "Catch!"

Of course, the brother did not "catch" and both pairs of my sacred socks fell into the tub.

Now, I know they were just socks, but at that moment in time, they were bigger than foot covers to me. I turned to the guilty sock thrower and with all the eloquence I could muster from four years of an education degree, I managed to say three words, "Get! Go! Leave!"

Yes, I saw the sunken face of my little guy as he ran down the stairs trying not to cry until he was out of my earshot. I knew I would go to him soon, but first I had to retrieve my socks from the bathtime bubbles.

While I was wringing the socks, my son was wringing his hands. He was downstairs crying. When my peacekeeping daughter went up to him and asked him why he was crying, he replied, "Mommy said I have to leave."

I had, of course, meant for him to leave the bathroom. He thought I wanted him to leave the house. All because he threw the socks into the bathtub.

I had to wonder what mental picture he was taking of this moment. Of course, with my luck, this picture will not be a snapshot. It will be a poster-sized blow-up that will completely cover all the wallet-sized memories of sweet moments.

I guess we never can know what our children are taking away with them from these days of their childhood.

The only thing we can do is hope that the memories of the good will balance out our less than best efforts.

I'm going to try to remember that everything that comes out of my mouth is going into the ears of the ones I love more than life itself. I need to watch what I say, how I say it and why I say it. Naturally, it would be much easier just to buy more socks.

What

Parents

Know

by

Heart

WATER BALLOONS

Filling up one hundred and twenty water balloons can give you a lot of time to think.

This was the conclusion I came to the other day when I realized I had but one thought on my mind: "Why is it that every year I look forward to summer vacation?"

Every year it is the same thing. Both the kids and I start excitedly counting down the days until school is out. "Only ten more days . . . only five more . . . only two!" And then that magical day arrives and the school doors close for three whole months. It is then that I have my one thought for the summer: "What was I thinking?! Why was I excited?"

Summer vacation means that I now have four kids at home full time. Four breakfasts—four lunches—four dinners. And snacks. And friends. And snacks for friends. I no longer have a kitchen, I have a twenty-four-hour diner. What is more, I am not sure why I ever thought I needed a pantry—the local grocery store is my pantry. It got so bad that the other day, during what would be my third trip to the store in one day, I walked past the produce man spraying the vegetables who greeted me with, "Weren't you just here?"

I then felt compelled to explain to him what it was like to have four kids at home full time during the summer—about the food—the demands—the chaos. But halfway through my tiring tirade, I noticed the produce man anxiously eyeing his vegetable sprayer and then looking back at me. At that point I decided I had better pay for my purchases and I headed home, clutching my Twinkies a little too tightly.

Maybe the produce man could not fully understand the pressure of having four kids at home full time during the summer. Of course, that is not quite the way it is in reality. The truth is that it would be a lot easier if they all were at home full time. But instead, each presupposed lazy day of summer is filled with swim lessons, swim team practice, soccer camps, cheerleading camps, birthday parties and play dates. When I am not in my kitchen or at the grocery store, I can be found behind the wheel of my mini-van, chauffeuring one or more child to one event or another.

And this is the state of mind I was in when I was pondering the summer while filling up a hundred twenty water balloons. It had been one of those days that started early and would end late. What is more, there was a swim team party at the pool that night that I had, of course, agreed to help run. And so it was that after dropping off the one hundred and twenty cans of pop for the party, I sat hunched over my backyard hose in the ninety-degree heat, filling up those water balloons for the ever-popular water balloon toss. As I realized I had not even had time to take a shower that day, I had to stop and wonder if my kids—or kids anywhere for that matter—could possibly ever appreciate what all we do for them. And as I sat upright to tie what would be the eighty-fourth balloon that day, I noticed my youngest was intently staring at me. I could tell by his enthralled attention that he was about to say something that was very important to him. "Here comes some of that appreci-ation," I suspected. And then he spoke. "You're getting old. I can see it in your face."

Want to guess what I did with the eighty-fourth balloon?

SNOW DAY

I remember it well.

Waking early on a snowy morning, anxiously awaiting the miraculous moment when I heard there was no school for me. The feeling of relief was celebrated by bounding back into bed. No, this is not a memory from my childhood. It is one from my teaching career.

Somehow, though, the thrill of an unexpected snow day still carries on into my motherhood career. There is still that surge of adrenaline as the TV's scroll of school closings gets closer and closer to my children's school district. And then the name appears and for a brief moment I forget that I am not the one getting the day off and I feel happy. And then, reality sets in.

So it was with our "last hurrah of winter" snowstorm. This was even more exciting for the kids due to the fact snow days were supposed to have all been left behind when we turned the calendar over to March. Upon seeing the coveted cancellation, I tiptoed into my children's rooms to turn off their alarm clocks. I might as well have run through the house banging pots and pans.

I have discovered the best way to wake sleeping children is to let them know they do not have to get up for school due to snow. Within a half hour three out of my four kids somehow found out there was no school and were already discussing the snowmen, igloos and snow angels they needed to construct immediately, if not sooner.

Of course, the days of my children all frolicking merrily together in the snow are gone. Truthfully, I'm not even sure if they ever frolicked together, but I like the word, nevertheless. These days, though, a snow day translates into more free time to spend with their friends. My oldest received three phone calls for social engagements before she even got out of bed. Of course, being an adolescent, that means sometime before lunch.

Now, I am not sure how much snow we actually got on that day. I know there were many estimates on that question. For me, though, I have a simple way to calculate the snowfall. I look outside to see how much of the lawn mower is covered with snow. Now, I know, most people suggest putting those things away for the winter, but that is a bit pessimistic for us. This year, we optimistically left it out in full view, knowing spring is just around the corner.

Besides, it makes a great measuring system for snow. A couple of our snowfalls have only left the wheels covered. Once, the white stuff hid the entire mower except for the throttle. This week's snowfall, though, took the prize. Except for ominous handles peeking out of the snowdrift, the full camouflage mission was complete.

Thus, armed with the knowledge it was a full snow-mower day, the kids began to race through the house seeking stray mittens and boots that had earlier been retired. At last, three were bundled head to toe in enough gear to have scaled Mt. Everest. And off they went in the untouched snow of the backyard. I believe they might even have frolicked. This recreation lasted maybe fifteen minutes.

And then the youngest came in crying because he had fallen face down in the snow. The middle two were arguing about who threw the harder snowball. However, I could not play nurse or referee at that moment, because the phone rang for another social engagement for my oldest. At this point it was 9:00 A.M. In spite of the chaos of the once coveted snow day, we did survive. I think the only thought that kept me going on this "day off," was that spring really is just around the corner.

And I will be ready.

I know right where my lawn mower is.

44

CHAPTER FOUR:
The Crying Heart

The crucible is for silver, and the furnace
is for gold, but the Lord tests the heart.
—Proverbs 17:3

ERIC THE GREAT

On the day the world lost Princess Diana, my hometown lost a prince. Now, the media around the world did not cover this story. As a matter of fact, the immediate coverage of this death was a simple obituary in the local paper that ended with the tag line, "Please, no pink flowers."

You see, this prince was a little boy with an incredible soul whose name actually did translate to "prince."

His name was Eric Krenzke, and he was from Hilliard, Ohio. He was eight years old and very proud of his royal name. He was also very proud of his Beanie Baby collection. He had every new coveted Beanie except one. He desperately wanted a tie-dyed bear with a 1970s circular symbol around its neck. The name of this Beanie Bear was Peace. But Peace was not to be made available until September. All of Eric's friends tried in vain to find him this bear, but to no avail. They just couldn't buy him Peace.

But then, peace never did come easily to Eric. He came into the world prematurely and was never afforded the opportunity to stop fighting. One of the many diagnostic tests he was forced to endure from birth spit out the diagnosis of idiopathic dystonia—a muscular disease that eventually destroys all of the body's muscles, including its most important one, the heart.

Eric's heart, however, was strong in ways that had little to do with talk about muscles. This heart gave him the courage to attend school in spite of uncomfortable breathing or feeding tubes. This heart gave him confidence even after having to learn to walk all over again five different times in his very short life. His heart kept him living.

Truer still, his heart and his family kept him living. If Eric's will and determination impressed people, they never had to look far to see where it came from. When Eric was three, while dealing with the roller coaster ride of his illness, his parents learned their other son, six-year-old Bobby, had been diagnosed with the same rare disease.

Being told your only children share the same fatal disease is more than most of us can even pretend to comprehend. But Eric and Bobby's parents never lost whatever it was that managed to keep them going.

Bobby's death at the age of nine made Eric painfully aware of what lay ahead for him. While it would have been understandable for this child to rebel against this injustice dealt to him in the cards of life, he proceeded with the courage that belied his age. He planned his own funeral (hence, the "no pink flowers" mandate) and then went on living what was left to live. Reading everything he could get his hands on, playing Donkey Kong and collecting those Beanie Babies made him just like any other boy his age for at least a while.

Some days, though, it would get to be too much even for a guy whose name meant "prince." Once, when watching the animated video series *Happily Ever After,* Eric rationally acknowledged, "Mom, I don't get to live happily ever after, do I?" And with the strength and wisdom the rest of us hope to never have to use, his mother replied, "You'll live happily ever after, Eric. Just not the way we had planned."

On August 31, 1997, while the world was mourning its lost princess, two parents said goodbye to their last son.

At that moment, I believe the only possible thing that could have kept them going was to imagine the incredible heavenly reunion taking place for two young brothers.

And I believe also that there was a miraculous, pain-free grin on Eric's face as he allowed Bobby—just this once—to show him the way.

The search was over.

At last, he had found Peace.

COLUMBINE

It was a picture of a baby that made me cry.

I was at the downtown library chaperoning a field trip for my daughter's sixth-grade class, when I saw an innocent picture of a baby. And it made me cry.

We had gone to the library to work on their research papers. But there was something about this day that made everyone want to cry.

This was the day after the hideous Colorado school killings and everyone was walking around just a little numb.

I couldn't help but look around me at the children busily working on the projects and realize that they were only a few years younger than those thirteen children who had been murdered at school the day before. But I also had to face the fact that they were only a few years younger than the two killers as well.

Since this has happened I have so badly wanted to label the murderers as monsters. But the fact remains, the most important label we must recognize is that they, too, were children.

How can ones so young be filled with hatred so strong that they are driven to do something so horrid in a place we parents believed to have been a haven for learning?

Again, the picture of the baby haunts me.

Years ago, when I sent my oldest off to kindergarten for the first time, I was scared. I was scared about the real world finally touching the daughter I had been able to protect for five too short years.

But, truthfully, I was scared for the little hurts I feared my child would have to endure. I was worried some child would not want to sit next to her on the bus. I worried she would feel sad if chosen last for a team in gym class. I worried she might get her feelings hurt by a classmate.

I never thought to worry that another child might one day bring a gun to school and start shooting.

Every day, we parents must trust that the bus drivers who daily transport our children to and from school are physically and mentally healthy. We have to assume that the teachers educating our children are academically and morally good. We believe that all the students who attend school with our children are basically the same as ours.

But not all are.

And when children so dramatically fall through a societal crack as the children did at Columbine, the whole world can hear the thud.

Or bang.

For these reasons the picture of the baby made me cry. To think that a child enters this world full of promise and purity and somehow makes such a wrong turn on the journey that is their life is more than I can bear.

I stare at the picture for the last time. I see the small pouting lips attempting a smile. I notice the soft, full head of dark hair. I smile at the full, rosy cheeks. And then I close the book, trying hard not to notice the caption beneath the picture:

"Austria, 1889. Adolf Hitler."

THE FIRST DAY

I knew there would be tears on the first day.

Yes, that first day finally arrived. The day that seemed like it would never come actually came and went.

My youngest started preschool.

Now, this may not seem like groundbreaking news to anyone else, but to me it was monumental. The day my baby began a three-afternoon-a-week preschool marked the first time in twelve years when I would have a block of time to myself in the course of my day.

People would often ask me if I was sad about this rite of passage. Trying to stifle my incredible glee, I would answer that I was pretty okay with it. And then I would try not to burst into giggles as I imagined my newfound free time beckoning me to come and play.

Truthfully, though, by the time this fourth baby of mine entered school, I was grateful to have a way to alleviate the guilt that comes with realizing your last baby doesn't have anything to call his own. He was always brought along to others' soccer games, lessons, plays and programs. He was also always the tagalong little brother for his brother's friends.

It amazes me to remember when I had my first baby. I think I had not even delivered her into this world before I set up her first play date. I couldn't wait to find friends for my firstborn. But my fourth had built-in playmates in his brother and sisters so I never felt the need to expand his social realm. Right before preschool started, he was planning his fourth birthday party. When his older brother commented about the skimpy invitation list, my little one unknowingly fanned the flame to this fire of

guilt in me when he answered, "But I don't have any friends."
And so we began our quest for friends in the form of planning
for preschool. Now, as you can imagine, this little guy who had
never been invited over to play with a friend and therefore
never had to leave his mommy for any length of time, might
have a problem with saying "goodbye" on that very first day. I
knew to be prepared for major tears. In fact, I had braced
myself for a major scene that might involve anything from des-
perate hand clutching to actual kicking and screaming.

Then the day arrived. His shiny backpack, which had been
waiting by the door for two weeks, was at last placed on his
back. Then, as I waited for the tears, he smiled proudly for the
obligatory first day of school photo. And I waited for the tears.
He climbed into the car with the zest of an astronaut boarding
his shuttle for the long-awaited flight. But I still was waiting
for tears. I peeked at his reflection in the rearview mirror as I
drove. His expression exclaimed the unspoken words, "It's
finally my turn!"

Now, at this preschool, you can drive the children up to the
waiting teacher who gets them out of the car and helps them
up the steps and into their room. As we got closer to the front,
I could see my son eagerly taking in his entire surroundings.
And it was here that I stopped waiting for his tears. For as he
kissed me goodbye and jumped out of the car, I had to watch in
wonder at this big-little guy who was so ready to be a part of
the world. And as my baby proudly took each step into his very
own school, he paused for just a moment to look over his tiny
shoulder only long enough to give me a smile and a slight wig-
gle of his fingers. And when the preschool door shut, blocking

What
Parents
Know
by
Heart

my view, the only sound in my car was the pounding of my very own heart. And that is when I came to realize I was right all along.

I knew there would be tears on the first day.

FRIENDSHIP

Children are blessed with the ability to collect friends like they collect seashells during a vacation at the beach. But just as they recognize how remarkable it is to discover a flawless sand dollar, they, too, are able to know when one friend stands out as a true treasure.

I have been thinking a lot about childhood friendships this week because this is an eventful week in my middle daughter's young social life.

This social life began when I first had to place her on the kindergarten bus at the ripe old age of five. We had just moved from Columbus to Cincinnati and I was due to have my fourth child within a couple of weeks. My daughter was not overly thrilled with any of these new changes in her little life—especially the part about going to kindergarten. And so she decided to run away from me right as the bus pulled up to take her to her second day of school. To fully appreciate this scene of a very pregnant woman chasing a five-year-old around the neighborhood, picture in her arms a two-year-old child as well. With my determined waddle overcoming her nervous dash, I finally caught my fleeing daughter and convinced her to get on the waiting bus. Tearfully she took her seat beside another little girl whose big brown eyes had taken in the whole ordeal. As the bus pulled away, the little girl sprouted the bud of a blossoming friendship with the simple words, "Hi. I'm Paige."

From that first encounter, the girls would go on to share kindergarten, first, second and third grades. But more importantly they shared secrets, giggles, dreams and the dawning revelation that boys might not really have cooties after all. And they

What
Parents
Know
by
Heart

also share necklaces. Each girl wears a different frog charm around her neck with indiscernible words that only when put together make up the phrase "Best Buds."

But this week the "Best Buds" will be separated. Paige is moving to the other side of the moon. Truthfully, she is moving to Texas, but when you are nine years old and your best friend for half your life is leaving, it might as well be into outer space. The girls have dealt with this fairly well up to this point. For up until now, the move has been too far into the future to be an actual reality. There were soccer games to be played, school work to be done, swimming meets to swim and boys to pretend they didn't care about. Now, however, the never arriving moving date has arrived.

And my daughter is starting to understand that Paige, her treasure of a friend, is honestly going to get in that moving van and leave.

I have tried to explain to her that this is just one chapter in her life. There will be many, many others.

But as she clutches her frog necklace there are tears in her eyes. And I understand. For when all is written in that book of life, I am sure my daughter will have numerous chapters of friends. Nevertheless, I am certain, for her, there will only be one Paige.

CHAPTER FIVE:
The Laughing Heart

. . . make a joyful noise before the king,
the Lord.
—Psalm 98:6

THE BOO-BOO BRAIN SYNDROME

Let me see if I understand this.

A study recently was published that comes to the conclusion that children whose parents both work outside the home have just as good brain function as children who have a parent at home at all times. The study looked at the areas of language, academics, behavior and self-esteem.

Well, I think it is wonderful for working parents to find comfort in this knowledge, but I feel the more obvious question was not even studied.

What about studying the brain function of us stay-at-home moms? We are a group who is begging for someone to study our brains. Actually, most days we are just begging for somebody over the age of five to talk to us.

I personally have realized this need for adult conversation by experiencing what I call a brain trance while catching what I believe is only a fragment of a daytime talk show that I simply cannot stand. Like a moth drawn to a flame, I soon find myself blankly staring at the TV screen, absentmindedly taking in the whole program, oblivious to the fact that my mouth is wide open the entire time.

And so, in the name of science, I have taken the four areas of the developmental study and I have selflessly offered up my own stay-at-home brain for observation.

Language Development: Who among us at-homers has not at least once marveled at how our language has changed in our new career? You can always tell another mother in a conversation due to her ease at discussing such things as spit up and the consistency of diaper deposits while never missing a bite of lunch. We refer to all pain, regardless of the severity, as a "boo-boo." And we have completely forgotten all grown-up words for body parts and functions.

Academic Achievement: You truly realize you are starved for intellectual stimulation when you notice the sole outlet for your inquisitive nature is to watch *Teletubbies* with a journalistic zeal, in your quest to find out what makes Tinky Winky tick.

Behavior Problems: A stay-at-home mom is called that very thing because she can never leave the role of mom far behind. On very rare occasions, when I might actually find myself out to dinner with a group of adults, I have to tightly clasp my own hands together to keep from cutting up the meat of the people seated next to me. And if someone excuses himself to go to the restroom, I begin to blurt out, "Do you need any help?"

Self-Esteem: It does do something to your sense of worth when you realize the total success of your day is directly dependent upon the quantity and quality of naps your little one has taken. What is more, you know you have hit a new low on the self-esteem ladder when you vaguely remember having taken a college course on persuasive reasoning, but are now reduced to using only the mother of all reasons: "Because I said so."

With this data presented, I encourage researchers everywhere to investigate this area where I feel brain function is suffering the most. I suggest calling it something scientific, like "The Boo-Boo Brain Syndrome."

But truthfully, the most mind-boggling fact of all is that in spite of the above mentioned research, most of the time we moms wouldn't trade our jobs for anything in the world.

And how do I know this is true?

Because I said so.

What
Parents
Know
by
Heart

Oh, Holy Plight

Sunday morning used to find me with my bags packed.

No, I wasn't going on a trip.

I was taking my family to church.

You know the drill.

The wake-up call.

The bombardment of breakfast.

The quest for clean clothing.

And then the packing of the diaper bag: bottles, diapers, wipes, cereal, toys, blanket and arts and crafts for the toddler in the group.

And there I stood, armed and ready for a spiritual journey.

Yeah, right.

Unfortunately, after the marathon morning of getting us all to church, usually the only praying I actually found myself doing was to pray that no one realized that incredibly loud sound came from one of my children.

But, that was before.

In our church, they offer childcare during services only in the form of a preschool and kindergarten program when the child is old enough to attend.

My youngest two were finally old enough to go to these classes instead of wiggling their way through worship.

Retiring our back-of-the-church seats to those other families who still had to entertain little ones, my husband and I confidently walked to our new closer-to-the-front seats with our two older daughters.

Halfway through the hour, I began to feel a sense of peace. I was able to pay attention and realized the chaos of worship with wee ones was behind me.

Just as I allowed myself to rejoice in this relaxation, at my side I began to hear the strange sounds I usually hear only in the middle of the night following the words, "Mommy, my tummy hurts." Of course the noise was coming from my youngest daughter and was followed by the sound of splashing on the floor.

In a split second, my husband and I were left to silently decide whether to attempt to get her to the bathroom or to continue to have her heave on the floor.

And in that split second, my husband, hoping to suppress her reflex to retch, clamped his hand over her mouth.

Now, this is the same technique he uses when he waters the plants and places his thumb over the garden hose nozzle. This works well to project the water rapidly and with force.

This time, however, the intention was ever so different, but the result was unfortunately the same.

Sparing the gory details, suffice it to say, the lady in front of us was now somewhat touched by my child's less-than-heavenly heaving.

The rest of the details are a blur, but I do recall ending the services on my knees. Not, of course, in prayer, but scrubbing the church floor.

And with the whole holy mess behind us, I had to laugh at the preposterousness of the ordeal. My youngest daughter now seems fine. Unfortunately, my older daughter is convinced we must change churches to salvage what may be left of our dignity.

Personally, I don't think it will go that far.

But, if you see a family of six making their way into your place of worship packing a spray can of disinfectant and a bucket, please be kind.

And try not to sit in front of them.

METEOR MOM

There was much written a while ago about a certain shuttle launch. It seems this was the first time a woman, namely Colonel Eileen Collins, was in charge. I applaud her effort on behalf of women everywhere. But also on behalf of women everywhere, I have one thing to say: "What's so surprising about that?"

All NASA had to do to see without a doubt that a woman is capable of handling incredible amounts of pressure is to hang out with a mom on earth for just one day. I am sure the NASA bigwigs would return from their day of childcare running with open arms back to their spacecraft.

Furthermore, if NASA had really wanted to see how different it would be to have a woman in charge of the journey, there was something they forgot. Where were the kids? When does a mom ever go anywhere without her entourage of offspring?

Now, that would have been something to talk about.

First, Meteor Mom would have to pack for her journey. Assuming Colonel Collins packed lightly for her five-day trip, multiply her luggage by forty-two if you are bringing along the kids. And then, naturally, although it may appear she has brought everything her children have ever owned in their entire lives, our space mom will not be able to find that very special blankie right before lift-off.

And speaking of lift-off, prior to this big moment, Meteor Mom will have asked her children approximately twelve times each if they had to go to the bathroom before they left. And quick as you can say "meteor shower," when the countdown reaches the big "0" one of them will have to go so badly they will be in danger of their own blast-off.

When that situation is under control, things will appear to be back on track for our mom in space. Then, one of the kids will mention they are in the Milky Way Galaxy, which will elicit cries from one of the other children upon remembering he did not have a snack yet.

None of this is too much for Meteor Mom, though, because she is used to it. She even anticipates it. For, when one child would start to torment another by whispering that he's a silly "asteroid," this mom knows how to nip the interplanetary name-calling before it even begins. She is, after all, at her zenith.

What is more, Meteor Mom can keep her sanity from going off into orbit even after listening to hours of knock-knock jokes that all end with the word *Uranus*.

Keep in mind, while all this is going on, our astronaut mom would still be manning the shuttle. Then again, maybe one should say she was *womanning* the shuttle.

And at the end of her journey, Meteor Mom would be feeling a sense of accomplishment and extreme pride at the enormous feat she had just achieved. This congratulatory moment, of course, would be interrupted by the screams of her youngest child, who just realized that the sighting of Pluto he had been promised on the journey was not the sighting of the dog of Mickey Mouse.

But Meteor Mom would manage it all. I would bet she could even do it all with a smile. Because she is a well-trained professional who is proud of her job.

She is a mom.

And there's nothing spacey about that.

THE CANINE CONNECTION

The pitter-patter of baby feet can again be heard at our house. No, we are not passing out cigars. We are handing out bones. We got a puppy.

Now, this is big news around here. We have never had a pet before. Even though my oldest would often quote statistics pointing to the fact that the majority of convicts in prison did not have a pet while growing up, we remained firm in our pet-free environment. Unless you can count fish as pets.

We had fine finned friends for many years, but with the exception of an occasional exclamation of, "Yuck! Look what came out of that fish," my children really never gave them much thought.

Still, when the last one of our fish did the belly-up back float in the water one day, I thought it would be traumatic for the kids. In my overly eager way, I organized an informal fish funeral in the backyard. At one point, with our dearly departed fish peacefully buried in his fish casket (otherwise known as a margarine container), I even had each of the kids put a rock across the freshly dug grave and say a little something. The first three said things as touching as "I will miss feeding you sometimes." Then it was my youngest's turn to eulogize. He walked over to the tiny gravesite, put his rock in place and said, "Now we can get a puppy. Amen."

And so we did.

The day our furry friend arrived was a big day. My husband went to pick up our new family member while everyone was anxiously waiting by the door. Everyone, that is, except me. I had come down with the stomach flu two hours before the

What Parents Know by Heart

puppy arrived. As daddy walked in the door with the puppy carrier, the children noticed a strange, yet familiar, odor coming from the crate. It seems the little pup was very afraid of the car ride and did what little pups do when they get very afraid. And during the ride, the new addition had lost his balance, fallen and obviously rolled into that which little pups do. Needless to say, when the coveted canine finally emerged from his carrier, our little white puppy was not so white. Thus, the argument over who first got to hold him, quickly ended.

After a bath and several outstretched arms later, he seemed to actually be comfortable in his new home.

And then the night arrived.

I realized I really didn't know anything about taking care of puppies. Everyone said to trust my mothering instincts. But when my babies would wake up at night, I would put them in bed with me and nurse them. Somehow I knew that wasn't the answer this time.

So at one point during that first night, in an attempt at canine comforting, I found myself lying on the floor in the basement, next to a whimpering baby dog, my stomach still cramping from the flu. In my infirmity, I started to dream I had gone through labor again. I may even have begun to lactate.

But now we have had the little white ball of fluff for a whole month and I think he is making himself right at home. As a little dog, he doesn't get into a lot of trouble yet except for the constant biting, and mistaking our carpet for the grass in the backyard. The only time he actually barks is when he sees something scary, like a vacuum cleaner. There is something about a sweeper that sends him into a barking frenzy every time. Because I have such concern for the little puppy, I have gallantly given up housecleaning.

Now, thanks to our new addition, I am happy to report that my children will not be destined for life in prison. What is more, they now have a pet with a bigger digestive track at which to marvel.

And somehow I feel safer. His breed may not be known as a watch-dog type, but I take comfort in knowing that we will now be alerted to any intruder who might try to enter our home.

Assuming, of course, the intruder is armed with a vacuum cleaner.

65

What

Parents

Know

by

Heart

DRIVES ME CRAZY

Someone once said it would be a good idea if there were a required license for becoming a parent. I venture to say that there is such a mandatory license. And that license is a driver's license.

The dawn of the new spring season has made it dawn on me that I spend most of my day in a car. Not, of course, driving myself where I need to go, but most likely driving my kids where they need to go.

With three soccer teams, a track team, one cheerleading squad schedule and a talent show rehearsal, I have now spent so much time in my car that I am considering hanging curtains in the back window.

Factor into that driving force the usual preschool, elementary and middle school drop off and pick up routines and you can readily see why I have just ordered one of those cute little chauffeur hats.

There is, however, something worse than having to spend the entire day chauffeuring kids, and that would be not having a car. And so it was that I ignored that piercing whistle my car was making for two weeks until it got so bad that the neighborhood dogs started chasing me. I made the appointment to take my car to the shop early one morning.

Now, my mechanic, Tony, is always so sweet to offer his customers a ride back home, but I had another plan that day. Have you ever seen those people who go out for a morning jog? Some of them have pets in tow and others have children in joggers. They look so fit and healthy. Well, I'm not one of those people. I've always thought about becoming an early morning jogger.

But so far, the closest I have come to a morning workout is when my kids forget their lunch boxes on their way to school, and I chase after them in my bathrobe.

So, I decided to turn the lemon of a broken car into the lemonade of a cardiovascular run. I graciously turned down Tony's offer of a ride home, pulled my stroller out of my broken van, put my youngest in the stroller and my dog on his leash. Thus began the first step of my new fitness routine, which was to be a two-mile jog home.

My pace was brisk. The morning air was refreshing. I managed to jog for two whole minutes before my son started whining that he wanted to walk. I stopped long enough to attempt to reason with a child who had never before shown an inclination for reason. This time, though, simply informing him of the hideous perils of the busy road we were close to bought me some more jogging time. For about another thirty seconds.

Then it was the dog's turn to break my stride by doing what dogs do when they are outside . . . or inside, if you're my dog. Thus I stopped long enough to bag the doggie dividend and continue on my way to fitness.

This time my gait was halted by the one in the stroller who had to be certain that the doggie bag I was taking back home was not actually touching his stroller in any way, shape or form.

By this time, I was indeed, sweating, but it had nothing to do with exercise. Taking a deep breath and a running start, I tried once again to be one of those joggers I so admired. The spring wind in my face felt good. The scent of the blossoming flowers permeated my steady breaths of air. My legs hit the sidewalk in a steady rhythm. Of course, then the front wheel of my stroller broke off. Completely.

Luckily I had not been going nearly as fast as I thought I had been, so the jolt of the broken wheel was minimal. But now I was left with a broken stroller, a four-year-old, a dog and a smelly doggie bag. Someone asked me why I didn't just pitch it and I had to say it was because it held sentimental value for me. I am, of course, referring here to the stroller, not the doggie bag.

I asked my son to walk now, but because I had done such a terrific job of scaring him about the dangers of the traffic, he tenaciously clung to the broken stroller out of fear of being turned into road kill.

So it was that I finished the last mile and a half of my planned workout doing an awkward walk with the child in the stroller propped up on its back wheels. This insured that the broken wheel did not touch the ground and the doggie bag, naturally, did not touch the child.

And so, I hold strongly to my belief that one does, indeed, need a license to have a child.

But with or without a license, there is always something to drive you crazy.

The
Book
of
Mom

FAIRY INTERESTING

Wanted: A new tooth fairy.

The old one seems to be getting a little long in the tooth.

I came to this conclusion last week, when my first grader finally lost the tooth that had been hanging, begging to be pulled for a week. It was so loose that it finally came out at a friend's birthday party while he was eating ice cream.

My little one was delighted about this dental incident as he put the newly pulled tooth in a plastic bag. It then went where millions of baby teeth in the past have gone before—under a pillow to anxiously await the tooth fairy's arrival and her donation of a certain small but exciting denomination of money.

The next morning, my son greeted me with a perplexed look on his face as he asked, "Mommy, guess what the tooth fairy put in my bag?"

Picking my chin up off the floor, I asked the hopeful question I already knew the negative answer to. "A dollar, like usual?"

"No," he managed a confused smile that showed his new gap. "She put my tooth back in the bag where it already was."

Now you see why I am seeking a new tooth fairy. The old one's just not as dependable as she once was.

There was a time, when my first child lost her first teeth, that a mistake like that never would have happened. No, those were the years the tooth fairy was so on the bicuspid ball that she would not only come when expected, but the little pixie would often leave a cute little note as well. Now the tiny imp can't remember a simple drill: take the tooth and leave the money.

Thus we need a new tooth fairy at our house. No experience is necessary. You might say we would be willing to have the den-

What
Parents
Know
by
Heart

tal elf learn from us while cutting her fairy teeth. She can come with or without wings, too. The only requirement is that she must have a better memory than the last one.

And that's not saying much.

Interestingly enough, we did come up with an explanation of what happened on that fairy-free night. Someone had to take the blame. And being the mature mother that I am, I told the tooth . . . I mean truth: The dog did it.

Yes. It was all on the conscience of the canine. I explained to my son that I was sure I had heard the dog bark in the middle of the night and he must have scared the tooth fairy away. And this theory was validated a short while later when another bark was heard as soon as my son went downstairs for breakfast. Sure enough, when the gap-toothed boy ran back upstairs, there was a dollar in the old plastic bag.

My son liked his dollar, but he was absolutely thrilled with this new story he could share with the entire first grade.

And while this tooth tale ended without a biting conclusion, I still am looking for a new tooth fairy. For I suspect that by the time my fourth child starts losing his baby teeth, the dog will be scaring away the old one, keeping her from fulfilling her dental duties over and over again.

So, if you or someone you know happens to be a tooth fairy with a great memory and a fondness for dogs, just let me know.

I hear it's a job you can really sink your teeth into.

Assuming, of course, you don't forget to look under the pillow.

No Lights

I have always been fascinated with the pioneers.

Okay, maybe I haven't always been fascinated with the pioneers. But I did watch *Little House on the Prairie* when I was growing up.

Things were so simple then. No machines constantly humming. No computers beeping for attention. No television sets continually talking.

I'm sure Ma and Pa Ingalls and their children bonded so well because there was no technology to steal their attention away from each other.

This was my first thought when the severe storm of last week literally left me in the dark. All right, maybe it wasn't my very first thought. My first thought was. "Please, let the lights come right back on." But when that didn't happen, I began to think of the pioneers.

Then again, they were not the first persons I thought of either. The first person I thought of was my husband, who was out of town on business and was going to miss the experience of such pioneer bonding with four kids stuck inside, during a storm, in the dark.

But once it was decided that the lights might not immediately pop back on, the kids and I went to the basement and talked about the pioneers and what we could do to pass the time.

"I want to play on the computer," came the first suggestion.

"Can we make some popcorn?" asked another.

"I want to watch a video."

Obviously, they were not quite the pioneers their mother was.

Finally we settled upon the idea of a progressive story. This is

What Parents Know by Heart

where one person starts the story and each of the others takes a turn adding on to the story. This worked well during my daughters' turns, but every time the story came to the boys, every character in the story began to suffer from seriously embarrassing bodily noises and then turned into a Pokemon.

But this activity did manage to get us into the second hour of our pioneer life without electricity. I patted myself on my pioneer back.

Then I prayed for the lights to come back on.

By this time we had with us several candles lighting the basement. The peaceful feeling candles usually give me was quickly substituted with the justified fear that someone would catch the house on fire.

And so I looked for yet another diversion. With this in mind, we started playing charades. This kept us going for a while in spite of the fact that my oldest and I were the only ones who really understood how to play this wordless game. When my four-year-old came up with the movie he entitled *Grandpa Is Singing* and was disappointed we couldn't figure it out, I knew it was time to stop.

We were now into hour three of our pioneer lifestyle.

The chaos in the basement was rising, along with the heat level due to having no air conditioning. The younger two were getting rambunctious and wrestling around the burning candles. The older two were scolding the younger two. I began to suspect the reason Ma Ingalls always wore a bonnet was that she had pulled all her hair out due to this pioneer bonding stuff.

It was then that it happened. In the candlelight of the basement, I had a vision of an idea. It was the dawning of an inspiration that almost glowed in the darkness.

Seeing the storm had subsided into the night, I grasped the pioneer spirit within me and told the kids to get in the car. Then I hooked up the little portable television that plugs into the cigarette lighter. And for one blissful hour we peacefully rode around town watching *Toy Story* on video.

I know what you're thinking.

But don't think for a minute that I wasn't still pondering the pioneers.

I imagine it was indeed something Ma and Pa Ingalls would have done.

They just didn't know how to plug the TV into the horse.

73

Mouse Madness

I have come to discover the term "quiet as a mouse" is highly overrated. At least at my house.

I came to this realization during an effort to appear to be keeping one of my New Year's resolutions. This resolution was to find some semblance of order in my house, and in keeping with this, we have all been cleaning out closets.

My girls, while reluctantly following this mom mandate, were the first to disprove this old adage, for they were also the first to detect tiny little brown specs in their closet. My husband got to be the one to inform them that what they saw was not bits of chocolate from their Halloween bag of candy that had been stashed among the shoes and sweaters.

No. It was a telltale sign. We had a mouse.

And the screams of disgust my girls managed to emit definitely were not along the lines of quiet as a mouse.

It took us another week to convince them that it was, indeed, safe for them to sleep in their room at night.

Unfortunately, we have come to discover that our rascal rodent is not working alone.

The other signs we have found throughout the house hint at a collaborative conspiracy.

We are all a little on the paranoid side to say the least.

The other day I was doing laundry. I blindly reached into the hamper to pull out the clothes. My hand completely encircled a small furry object.

I admit my reaction was not as quiet as a mouse.

But the object in question was, indeed, as quiet as a mouse. It was a Beanie Baby.

I fully expect my heart rate to be back to normal within the next few days.

With no other options in this war of mice and men, we set up a few mousetraps. We caught one mouse right away.

Again, the cries of protest from my oldest were far from the quiet of that expression. I couldn't fault her tenderhearted plea for humanity, though. After all, when I was her age, I interrupted a family vacation once by forbidding everyone around me to fish. It wasn't that I was worried about the fish—I was concerned for the right to life of the earthworms.

But that was then and this is now.

Even the dog is affected by it all. The other day he was barking and growling furiously. I ran to the room, fully expecting my canine conqueror to have cornered a critter. All I saw, however, was my dull-witted dog barking at his own reflection in a floor-length mirror.

As part of our rodent revolution, we have removed everything from our house that reminds us of these vagrant vertebrates called mice. The movies *Stuart Little* and *An American Tale* have been thrown out. Ditto for all Tom and Jerry cartoons. Just to play it safe, we are having the Disney channel taken out of our cable package next week.

Until then we have set up a few more mousetraps.

Unfortunately, the only thing we have caught in those so far is my husband's thumb when he was reaching for a grocery sack. Of course, when that happened, you can probably guess that the term "quiet as a mouse" never even entered my mind.

MR. SCHNOOKUMS

When I quit teaching to stay home full time after my second child was born, I fell into the supermom syndrome. I made myself believe I had to run a mini preschool for my two children. I planned daily crafts, field trips and science experiments to stimulate their growing minds. All of these occasions were dutifully recorded on video and in still pictures.

Thankfully, I quickly got over it.

But it was interesting for a while. For example, when my first-born was interested in caterpillars, I bought a little caterpillar farm that came complete with a netted cage and a place to send away for larva that would turn into butterflies. I admit it was fascinating watching nature unfold like that. We even had a big celebration party on the day we set our newly evolved butterflies free.

Today, when my third and fourth children catch something entirely on their own, I only go so far as to hand them an empty coffee can.

And so it was that my little boy came home from school one day with a prized possession that was crawling from one little hand to another. While it didn't look like much more than a fuzzy worm to me, to my son it held endless possibilities of evolving into the most beautiful creature ever.

Somewhere behind the dark valley of the cabinet under my kitchen sink, I was able to find an old coffee can. At this point with my firstborn, I would have pulled out all the books I had on caterpillars, cocoons and butterflies. But with this, my third child, I poked the holes in the lid, handed it to him and was finished.

I have to admit, though, my son made a nice little caffeinated cottage for his little critter. He even named his caterpillar Mr. Schnookums. Mr. Schnookums became a part of my middle child's life for five days. Everyday, before and after school, he would check on Mr. Schnookums who lived in the coffee can under the shade of an old vibernum tree.

Then it happened.

One day, taking a break in his day and coming home for lunch, my husband decided to water his garden—which happens to be next to the vibernum tree.

Two hours later, my little guy repeated his pattern of the last few days as he ran straight out to the coffee can under the tree. Only by this time, Mr. Schnookums's cute little home had suddenly become equipped with an indoor pool.

Seeing Mr. Schnookums doing the back float was not what my son had hoped for, but he remained unusually calm as he poured the water out of the can, taking Mr. Schnookums into his hands. I do believe he did a form of CPR (caterpillar pulmonary resuscitation). Incredibly, that little worm started to move again.

What a relief to know my husband would not be charged with insecticide this time.

We celebrated this resurrection by setting Mr. Schookums free into that vibernum tree. I would have taken a picture of this joyous occasion, but of course, I haven't had film in the camera since my fourth child was born.

What

Parents

Know

by

Heart

The Cookie Conspiracy

First, there was Oprah inviting us to "get with the program" and diet and exercise with her.

Then, there was Rosie O'Donnell suggesting we join her Chub Club and train for a 5k run.

My own fitness goals are not as dramatic as the dreams of these talk show diet divas. My admittedly modest ambition is that I would simply like to be able to carry my laundry hamper from the basement laundry room all the way upstairs without having to stop and catch my breath.

This year I was slowly working on that goal of laundry basket basics, and I felt I was making a little progress. But then it happened.

It is an annual February event that spells disaster to those of us who promised once more in our New Year's resolutions that we would get fit and eat healthier.

No, I am not referring to Valentine's Day as the culprit here. I actually can't even remember the last time I received a heart-shaped box of chocolates for this day of romance, but I think I was dressed to go out to a disco, so I think it's safe to say it was a while ago.

No, this time I am referring to the annual February fitness conspiracy commonly known as: the arrival of the Girl Scout Cookies.

Think about it. Every January, just as we are feeling confident about our New Year's resolution to shape up, these sweet girls brave the bitter cold to ring our doorbells and ask for our support of their worthwhile organization via ordering their innocent little cookies. And what is more, you don't even have to worry about paying for them or eating them until the next month.

And I'm not sure, but I believe there is a rule somewhere that says you cannot buy only one box of cookies. I seem to recall that the acceptable minimum order is three boxes per girl.

Multiply that statistic by the number of girls you and your children have ever known in your entire life, and you now have the number of boxes that will be waiting for you on that diet-devastating delivery day in February.

As of last week, due to this anti-fitness conspiracy, I have a mountain of Girl Scout cookie boxes stacked so high in my kitchen that I suspect when I actually get to the bottom of the pile, I will find a friendly Girl Scout patiently waiting to collect her money.

And as I begrudgingly trek through this valley of sweets, I am left with my shape-up plan completely bent out of shape due to the fact that Thin Mints are not the diet food I had hoped the name had suggested.

I think, however, that I have a solution that will cut out a lot of the time I spend worrying about this. Next year, when my cookie order comes, I will simply take the boxes and strap them directly to my waist, hips and other areas where they eventually would end up anyway.

And I plan to share this new idea with my friendly Girl Scout. Just as soon as I find her.

CHAPTER SIX:
The Holiday Heart

*For where your treasure is, there your
heart will be also.*
—Matthew 6:21

EASTER

On my way to meet a lady I was interviewing, I couldn't keep
my mind from racing about how unprepared I was for Easter. It
was less than two weeks away and no bunny decorations were
up at my house, no plastic eggs were filled with candy, and
there were no new clothes purchased for my children to wear
on the big day.

I pushed these thoughts aside as I greeted the woman I would
be talking to for the next two hours. Her peacefulness belied
the struggle she had just been through. She began her story by
telling me about a tiny plastic bag.

It was a simple plastic bag that the hospital had given her. She
hadn't come across it before in the last two months since it was
buried in her purse and, with three little children, she usually

only carries the diaper bag. But there it was. A plastic bag that contained, for her, a symbol of the brief months before as well as a symbol of her life now. For inside this bag was the figure of Jesus, broken off the cross of a rosary, alongside the wedding ring of her late husband.

And somehow this made perfect sense to her.

On December 5, 1999, John and Mary Dugan were getting ready for church with their three children, ages four, two and five months, when John noticed a tingling in his legs. By that evening, he would be in the hospital, paralyzed from the chest down. A rare diagnosis of transverse myelitis was made, as doctors recalled that people have only a one in a million chance of this happening. Within the next week, John began rehabilitation trying to regain what he had lost.

But, as amazing as what he had lost certainly was, what was even more amazing was what he did not lose: his humor, his thankfulness, his faith. His room became a testimony to the human spirit as he assured all who were concerned for him that his suffering had to have a purpose in the greater scheme. While he couldn't know the true reason, he did know that he had been chosen to carry this cross of suffering for some important intention.

His cross, however, was to soon get even heavier. On December 31, after only one day of a terrible cough, an x-ray discovered yet another rarity. John had contracted a fungal infection of the lungs that usually only occurs in the southeastern section of the United States. Somehow though, this infection, called blastomycosis, had found John. Within a couple of days, he would be on a ventilator, fighting for every breath.

Still, he embraced this suffering like no one could imagine. Over the next week, John's room would be continuously full of a chain of friends and family praying for him around the clock. People were coming with the intention of offering peace, but ended up leaving with a sense of peace like they had never known.

On January 10, 2000, at the age of forty-one, John Dugan, breathed his last breath of suffering. Like the Christ figure of the broken rosary Mary had found in her purse, he was free of his cross.

But Mary Dugan was left to carry her cross alone. She admits she will always carry this cross in one way or another. But she gets her strength from the way her husband lived as well as the way in which he died. And on those nights when her four-year-old gets out of bed because he misses his daddy, Mary assures him that she misses him, too. And then after a discussion about how heaven must have all the toys and food you ever loved, she tucks him in again telling him that now his daddy is able to love him perfectly.

And as she looks at the three small children that she and John brought into this world together, the burden of her own cross is somehow lightened by remembering the last conversation she had with her husband.

Going to see him early that last morning, Mary remembers John looking at an eleven-by-fourteen-inch picture of the children that had been tacked to his hospital wall. He explained how he had just watched the rising sun coming in through the window, rays of light illuminating each child, one at a time. And seeing the sun gently caressing each of his children but for that brief moment left him with the sense that he was being told they would all be fine.

And as I reflected on all they had been through as she discussed this beautiful assurance of life given to them through the rising of the sun, one thought came to me.

All at once, I felt ready for Easter.

FATHER'S DAY

"You look nice. Have a good day."

And thus began a typical school day for me.

It was the 1970s. I was on my way to school and my dad was driving.

Remember, if you will, that fathers of this time were of a different generation. Their sole concern was that there was enough money to clothe the family, feed the family and educate the family. It was the mother's job to raise the family.

Now, this is not to say that my dad was uninvolved with my siblings and me. We always knew he was there and never doubted the love.

But, nevertheless, my dad was not into reading books in order to pontificate on parenting practices. A typical scene at our house was one of dad reading the paper while mom was doing the dishes. As the volume of the frolicking children grew, my mom would come out of the kitchen long enough to request of my dad, "Please settle the kids." At which point he would calmly lower his paper just enough inches to say over the top, "Kids, settle."

For this reason, I enjoyed my rides to school with my daddy. Having him and his full attention to myself for five whole minutes was a treat that did not go unnoticed by me. And everyday it was the same routine. As we pulled into the school, I would kiss my parental chauffeur on the cheek, at which point he would say the lines I had grown to expect, "You look nice. Have a good day." And, I would echo those lines back to him as I exited the car, ready to start my day, full of the knowledge that my daddy thought I looked nice.

And this routine remained unchanged for years, with the small

*What
Parents
Know
by
Heart*

exception of when I started junior high school. This was the time I informed him I was going to kiss him goodbye while he was still driving, before we actually got to school. This, of course, was due to my adolescent anxiety, fueled by the fear my classmates might realize I actually had parents and, heaven forbid, even liked them.

But when the car stopped, it was still the familiar, "You look nice. Have a good day."

It was such a simple thing, but I am certain from that original exchange blossomed a belief that I was worth something. Years later, before I found my prince, while shuffling through many frogs, I remember on more than one occasion being displeased with something one of my dates might have said. The first thought to pop into my head was always, "My dad wouldn't treat me that way."

How true it is, that the first man in a little girl's life is her daddy.

And now I watch my dad with my children. To say he cannot get enough of them is an understatement. There is definitely no reading of the newspaper when the grandkids visit. He doesn't want to miss a minute this time around. His favorite shirt is one that says, "If I had known how much fun having grandkids would be, I'd have had them first."

But something tells me he wouldn't have given up all those rides to school either.

So, this Sunday for Father's Day, I know just what I'll do. I am going to go right up to my dad and proudly say, "You look nice. Have a good day." And then I will kiss him on the cheek.

No matter who is watching.

REAL BOOS OF HALLOWEEN

Ah . . . the sounds of Halloween.

The autumn leaves crunching under the feet of costumed trick-or-treaters.

Eerie organ music reverberating down every decorated hall.

Kids crying.

Okay. Maybe that last one isn't among everyone's selected sounds of the season. But it always pops up in mine.

"Mom!" my oldest whined. Truthfully, the moan is more of the two-syllable "Mah-um" variety. "I absolutely have to be Britney Spears for Halloween. Everyone I know is dressing like her and I just have to be Britney!"

Because my daughter's bedroom door is practically wallpapered with pictures of that particular young singing sensation, I happen to know how Ms. Spears dresses. I would have had the costume ideas covered. Unfortunately the costume itself would not cover enough. You see, Britney's signature statement (if one, indeed, can have a signature statement at her young age) is to always show her midriff. Dreading the thought of my adolescent sprinting through the neighborhood showing more skin than common sense, I said, "No."

"But, mom," she retorted, this time with no whine, just adult-like reasoning, "I have thought a lot about this for a long time. Haven't you ever wanted to dress up like someone famous?"

With that question, she had pulled out the heavy artillery. Suddenly it wasn't my daughter's face I was staring at any more, but rather my own much younger face looking back at me. I flashed back to a Halloween of twenty-some years earlier when some friends and I wanted to go as the Partridge family.

What
Parents
Know
by
Heart

Of course, we all wanted to be Laurie Partridge. And frankly, we had no idea what our costumes would consist of other than braces that we had hoped would pick up radio waves. But this costume never came to be. I had to go as a gypsy that year.

Somehow, by agreeing to allow my daughter to appear on Halloween as a singing teen machine, Laurie Partridge would live on. Yet, somehow, by agreeing to allow my daughter her teen dream, I realized my most difficult job lay ahead of me: telling her daddy about her selection.

Now, the picture he holds in his mind of the perfect costume for our daughter is most likely the red, baggy clown suit she wore as a toddler. The picture my daughter has on her door shows that Britney definitely does not believe in baggy.

And so I avoided this coming confrontation by personally agreeing to sew a teen sensation costume that an adolescent would think was worthy, and an adolescent's dad would think sufficient to ward off frost bite on a cold All Hallows Eve.

With that Halloween hoopla settled, I hit the fabric store and then began to conjure up this mythical costume. Midway through my third attempt at this parental project, my younger daughter burst into the room.

She has had her ice skater costume ready for over a month. I got it on sale and then spent hours drawing ice skates on foam boards that would cover her tennis shoes as she trick-or-treated. The finished costume was well worth the time, though. And now I was certain she had come in to tell me how much she appreciated my efforts.

"I changed my mind," she stated matter-of-factly. "I want to be Britney Spears, too."

Because I literally was sitting on pins and needles, I was finally able to toughen up and push the Partridge family right out of my mind. That gypsy costume was pretty good after all.

I informed her that her costume was not going to change.

Of course, she began to cry.

Ah . . . the sounds of Halloween.

THE PUTRID PUMPKIN I

Some traditions you embrace with your whole heart.

Others you wish you had never started.

The latter was my thought the day before Halloween.

Several years ago—when I had only two children, I started the tradition of buying a pumpkin for each one to design. I would, of course, have to do the carving myself.

This was a fun family moment that we enjoyed.

And then there was another child and another pumpkin to carve.

And then another child, and yet another pumpkin to carve.

As if four pumpkins to carve in one night were not enough, in my infinite maternal wisdom (a.k.a., delusion) last year I bought one of those pumpkin-carving kits. These are the ones that allow you to carve intricately detailed designs on your pumpkin. The final results leave you with a mini-masterpiece of prime pumpkin. Once again, the kids did the choosing of the designs and I did the actual carving.

I estimate that it took me more time to carve jack-o-lanterns and bring those pretty pumpkins into this world than it did to deliver all four of my children combined.

So, this year I had hoped to avoid that pumpkin pandemonium. A couple of weeks before Halloween, I bought one and only one beautiful pumpkin.

Proudly I put it on the porch to await the delighted squeals of my children upon returning from school that day.

"Where are the other ones?

"Is that one mine?"

"Why is there only one pumpkin?"

When I suggested we just do one nice family pumpkin this year, you would have thought by the looks on their faces that I had told them everyone was passing out apples instead of candy this year for trick-or-treat.

And so it was that I agreed to buy more pumpkins.

But between soccer games, play practices, football games, swimming lessons and life in general, two weeks flew by without my thinking too much about our pumpkin predicament.

Then one of my kids noticed something about the one pumpkin we did possess.

"Hey, did you know the pumpkin smells and is soft in the back?"

So with a moldy pumpkin on my porch, the kids and I set out to buy four non-moldy pumpkins so this tradition could continue and my children could grow up to be happy well-adjusted citizens.

Of course by now it was the day before Halloween. And thanks to the new time change, we had only one hour of daylight for our search.

The first store did not have one pumpkin left.

The second store did not have one pumpkin left.

Ditto for the third and fourth stores as well.

Soon, that moldy pumpkin on our porch was looking better and better to me.

Unfortunately, though, it didn't smell better to me. Have you ever cut into a moldy pumpkin? To describe it as unpleasant would be a compliment. But I was bound and determined that there would be at least one jolly jack-o-lantern on my porch for my children to enjoy.

And so I sat outside in the dark, carving my moldy pumpkin

while the aroma literally made tears come to my eyes.

After what seemed to be much more than the forty-five minutes that it actually took, I was almost finished with my pumpkin project.

Sure it smelled hideous. Sure, my hand poked through the soft, moldy back. Sure, my kids were all inside, completely uninterested.

But this was one tradition that I had salvaged by sheer determination.

Then my hand slipped, completely taking off the detailed nose I had been carving as the final touch. Now, I had nothing but a big hole in a putrid pumpkin.

Some traditions you embrace.

Some traditions you wish you had never started.

And some traditions simply stink.

THE PUTRID PUMPKIN II

Lately, I have been thinking a lot about Linus.

You know Linus. He's the thumb-sucking, blanket-holding little boy from the Charlie Brown *Peanuts* series.

Now, normally I do not go around contemplating cartoon characters. But lately I have. I have been thinking about Linus.

Specifically, I have been thinking about Linus and his quest for the Great Pumpkin. Remember that Halloween special? Little Linus faithfully sitting in the pumpkin patch waiting . . . hoping . . . persisting in his pursuit to find the Great Pumpkin.

Except for the thumb-sucking part, that has been me.

In the previous story I described my family's tradition of carving pumpkins and how my procrastinating one Halloween postponed our pumpkin purchasing so late that all I was left with was a rotten, putrid pumpkin. I finally got the smell off the front porch around New Year's Eve.

Well, the next year I made my children a pumpkin promise. I vowed that we would not wait until the last moment to purchase our pumpkins. This year would be different.

And so it was that one whole week before Halloween that year I took my kids to a pumpkin patch. Okay, truthfully it was a makeshift pumpkin stand in a parking lot of a strip mall close to my house. But somehow that just doesn't set the tone for the story as well as the phrase, "pumpkin patch."

Arriving at our modern pumpkin patch, I breathed a sigh of relief upon seeing a vast sea of orange fruit surrounding us. Indeed, this year would be different.

Each of the kids was given the task of picking out his or her own pumpkin from this sea of possibilities. And each waited for

93

What
Parents
Know
by
Heart

the other to choose first. No, this was not a display of great manners. The hesitation in selection was simply due to the fact that each wanted to be sure her or his own pumpkin was bigger and better than his or her brothers' and sisters' pumpkins, and the only way he or she could be assured of that was to pick hers or his out last.

After enough time to have selected a life-long mate, my children finally had their pumpkins picked out. We headed home to a rising chorus of, "Can we carve them tonight? Can we carve them tonight?"

But since it was a school night, I had to rain on their jack-o-lantern parade and inform them we had to wait until the weekend to carve them.

My six-year-old was particularly proud of his picked pumpkin. He had, indeed, been able to select his last of all and was more than pleased with his prize.

He gave his pumpkin a bath before leaving it on the front porch. I thought for a moment he was going to ask to sleep with it that night.

As it turned out, I wish he had.

As the kids walked out the door the next morning for school, we quickly realized that something was missing. Four things, to be exact. Our pumpkins were gone.

Somewhere in the course of the night, a pumpkin pirate must have come to our house. I can only assume this pirate had a mother who most likely was never able to purchase pumpkins promptly—thereby leading her or him to this life of pumpkin pilfering.

I managed to keep the tears of my disappointed kids away with the promise that we would buy four more pumpkins the first chance we got.

Unfortunately, the first chance we got was the day before Halloween. And the sea of orange was gone. My little parking lot patch had closed up shop. I drove on and on. Finally I found one pumpkin. Again, there was only one pumpkin left in the city. And do you want to guess what it smelled like when we cut it open?

So once again I was left to carve a putrid pumpkin while vowing that next year would be different.

Now you can see why I have been thinking so much lately about little Linus and his quest for the Great Pumpkin.

Yes, I can really relate to the little guy. As a matter of fact, I suddenly have the urge to suck my thumb.

And I would, too.

Except for the fact that my thumb still stinks.

95

What

Parents

Know

by

Heart

THE SANTA PAUSE

Why are we all in such a hurry?

It's bad enough that I had to endure my first Christmas commercial even before I had smuggled my first candy bar from the kids' trick-or-treat bags.

But, now I am noticing this fast-forward philosophy spilling over into my children's childhood everyday.

Hollywood knows how to push our children's fast-forward buttons. Movies that used to be innocent fun for the whole family are now being remade with a rating of PG-13. I envision the next big release for these studios to be *The New Adventures of Mother Goose*—Parental Guidance Suggested.

Technology helps us push that fast-forward button, as well. I had to laugh the other day when I was looking for a computer program for my four-year-old (okay, I admit there are fast-forward button imprints on my own finger, too), and there was a program called *Jump Start Baby*. Since when do children need a computer program to get ready to be babies? I didn't look at the skill levels of the program, but I was left to imagine headings such as "Spit Happens" and "The Do's and Don'ts of Diapers."

Why are we all in such a hurry?

At no time is that question more in my mind than during the Christmas season. This is because that is the time when children all over the world ask their parents the big question.

No, this question is not about the birds and the bees.

This question is about Santa and the elves.

You see, even other children know how to push that old fast forward button.

When my oldest child was in second grade her heart was broken when her first-grade best friend told her there was no Santa Claus.

In tears, she came to me and asked if this was true.

Taking a breath and trying to remember every line to "Yes, Virginia, there is a Santa Claus," I stopped myself before my dissertation began and I simply asked, "Do you want to believe?"

In a heartbeat, she nodded her answer, "Yes."

"Then, believe," I replied.

She smiled as the simplicity of my command sunk in, but her eyes began to narrow with thought as she spoke, "Do *you* believe, Mommy?"

Wishing to take my finger off that fast forward button and hit the pause button instead, I answered her question with another question, "Why do we celebrate Christmas?"

"Because Jesus was born," she proudly stated.

"And because of his incredible birth," I continued for her, "the entire season holds such magic for me that I believe anything is possible. And I think that Santa represents all this magic for children to believe in. So, yes, I believe in Santa Claus."

Since that day, she has approached this age of awareness gradually and on her own. I suspect my second child also has her suspicions as well, but she's savvy enough to assume her present load could be reduced if she looks the gift horse in the mouth and then questions his existence. So far, she has not asked.

And I am satisfied to be sitting on the pause button this time. For when I see my children's eyes absolutely dancing with joy on Christmas morning as they open Santa's surprises, I really do believe.

And that is one magic moment I am in no hurry to forward.

CHRISTMAS WISH

I remember when I was a little girl and I would always ask my dad what he wanted most for Christmas. Every year it would be the same answer, "Peace on earth, good will toward men."

That seemed like a pretty tall order to fill for a kid. So I always bought him a package of handkerchiefs instead.

It has only been recently, though, that I understand what my dad was getting at. The older I get the more I realize that peace on earth and good will toward men is not so outlandish a request after all.

And we don't even have to go to the Middle East to achieve it, either.

We could start with our very own family.

The other day my two youngest were at a store that sells everything for ninety-nine cents, where they were doing their only Christmas shopping. After picking out most of their presents rather quickly, my boys asked me to hide my eyes while they searched for my gift. This proved to be a difficult task for the kid consumers. Finally, growing impatient with having to hide my eyes in public, I commented that I was sure they could find something I would like very much in the few minutes we had left, but could they please decide quickly. To that my little one announced, "But I don't want to hurry, Mommy—I want your gift to be the best one of them all."

It will be many years before he will realize that the precious gift he did, indeed, give me this year did not come with a bar code or price tag attached.

His words were wee steps toward peace on earth, good will toward men.

I had another reminder of my dad's Christmas wish this holiday season when my kids and I went to visit our friend who is in a retirement center. We wanted to take her something special, but what could she possibly want or need?

We arrived with a Christmas sweatshirt that was gratefully accepted. But I didn't feel that was quite it. Soon into our conversation, our elderly friend apologized for not being able to put up her decorations this year.

That was it.

That was all I needed.

Within fifteen minutes my kids and I had her room decorated from the meager two boxes of Christmas memories that we pulled from her closet.

Her tears of joy told us that this was the best present we could give her. We gave her ourselves.

Peace on earth, good will toward men.

I think maybe my dad was on to something here.

Truthfully, this is something we all know but we push aside because it is actually easier for us to go to a store to find our presents than it is for us to go deep inside ourselves to find the gifts we possess within.

But this Christmas let's remember, after the sweatshirts and handkerchiefs are all opened, let's decide to give a gift that only needs to be wrapped in our own arms.

Before the gifts of this special season give way to a memory once again, let us start giving gifts of the heart.

We can call it baby steps for peace on earth and good will toward men.

Let's give each other the gift of our love.

99

It's one size fits all.

And returns are not just allowed, they are absolutely encouraged.

The
Book
of
Mom

SEASON'S REASON

Something was missing.

I was going through the motions. I was playing all the parts. And still something was missing.

I'm talking about my Christmas spirit, here. Or lack of it.

Now, usually I am among the biggest kids I know at holiday time. My oldest will not even go shopping with me during this time of year, because all the stores are playing Christmas music and I cannot always be held to my promise of not singing in the middle of a department store. I mean, who can resist the urge to sing along with "Jingle Bell Rock"—even if your daughter and four of her closest friends are watching with their ears open?

But this year it hadn't happened for me yet. Something was missing.

Maybe it was because the holiday displays hit the stores before my kids had even hit the streets for trick-or-treating.

Whatever the reason for my lack of cheer, I knew I had better put on a happy face and get moving. There were cookies to bake, presents to buy and a house to decorate.

And it was during this last stage of events that I discovered something—or something was discovered for me.

My youngest and I were sorting through the musty boxes of stored decorations, accomplishing little more than inventory.

"Oh, I remember this!" he would gush as he pulled out each and every item that had made it through another year. "Do you remember this one, Mommy?" he would ask.

Now, this is the point where I would usually turn into a seasonal sentimental fool, picking up each ornament and recalling when, where and why it was purchased.

Not this year, though. There was just something missing.

What
Parents
Know
by
Heart

"I can't find it," my son's words, all at once, seemed to echo my own thoughts. "Where is it?" he continued as he not very gently pulled from the box various items that were obviously not what he had in mind.

"Where is it?" he intently repeated his inquiry. Before I could even ask him what it was he was seeking, his next statement answered more than one question for me.

"I found Jesus!" my son triumphantly declared.

Now, this was not so much a spiritual revelation for him as much as it was an actual discovery. He had finally found the manger scene.

"Is that what you were looking for?" I asked even though the answer was obvious.

"Yeah, Mommy. Look." His big brown eyes were dancing as he explained the rest. "He was right here the whole time. Only all this other stuff was covering him up."

If our lives came equipped with a soundtrack, at that very moment, the Christmas carols, for me, would have begun to fill the air.

"Thank you so much for finding him for me," I managed to say in spite of the cracking in my voice.

"Welcome, Mommy," he answered, oblivious to the actual discovery he had made.

And that is my holiday wish for you.

Whatever this season means to you, may you celebrate it with more meaning than ever before. But if somehow, throughout the years, you start to forget what that reason really is, I have but one suggestion:

Let a little child lead you.

Christmas Lights

When it comes to Christmas, my husband and I are in a mixed marriage.

Now, the difference is not in the way we celebrate Christmas. The difference is in the way we decorate Christmas.

And as with everything, this difference is rooted in our childhoods.

During our first Christmas, shortly after my husband and I were engaged, we went to visit my future in-laws. As we pulled up to their house, I stared into the darkness and asked, "When are your folks decorating for Christmas?"

"What do you mean?" my husband blankly asked. "They already did decorate."

Upon closer inspection—much closer inspection—I noticed there was, indeed, a single lit candle in each of their windows. And a green wreath on their front door.

My husband did not have to wait long to understand my confusion about his parents' understatedly decorated house. He only had to wait until our first Christmas visit with my parents.

Upon turning the corner that leads to their house, my husband-to-be had to shield his eyes from the glare. There were lights in the trees, lights on the bushes, lights on the rooftop. You name it and if it did not move, my parents hung a string of lights on it. My fiancé commented that he had seen fewer lights on the Vegas strip.

And so you can easily see that we came by our mixed marriage quite naturally.

But we have tried to deal with this Christmas quandary from the beginning of our marriage. We compromised. I decorated the inside of the house however I wanted and he decorated the outside however he pleased.

For the first few years my spouse went all out. He hung a wreath on the front door. Of course, I must mention there was a floodlight shining on this wreath for effect.

This worked until the kids were born and developed their own opinions—approximately fifteen minutes after birth.

"Our house looks boring." They would complain. "Santa won't even be able to find it. Please can we put up some lights?"

And so, little by little—one year at a time—I have been sneaking in a few decorative touches to our outside Yuletide decorations. One year it was simply a few red bows for the bushes. The next year, it was a few white lights for the bushes. My husband, of course, did notice the additions, but, wise man that he is, he knew he was outnumbered, and reluctantly gave in to this mutiny. But still the kids wanted more.

"Everyone else has those pretty icicle lights," they noticed one year. "Can we please get those?"

And so it was that I could recently be found precariously perched on a ladder next to a tree in our front yard, trying to hang a tangled tier of icicle lights. One hour later I had learned something important. You can't hang icicle lights from a tree.

And so, after another half an hour of untangling them from the tree, I decided to try to hang them from my house. I soon discovered another important point to remember. I have a two-story house, but only a one-story ladder. So, ever the diligent little elf, I thought I would simply drape the icicle lights across the middle of the house for a dramatic effect. Once more, I spent the better part of an hour attempting this. And after almost three hours total decorating time, it was finally done.

And as I stood in the yard, staring at my accomplishment, panting and yet proud of my new strand of lights—my youngest son came out to inspect my work. After looking quizzically at the new display for a minute, he honestly responded, "It looks like our house has a mustache."

The worst part was—he was right. The windows were the eyes—the front door was an open mouth—and my attempt at icicle lights had created an elaborate handlebar mustache for the Bundy abode.

I ripped the icicle lights down and put a wreath on the door. That took about five minutes.

Now, where do I find those darn candles?

105

New Year's Eve

While celebrating the tradition of Exchange Day, otherwise known as the day after Christmas, at a local mall, I happened upon a display of beautiful garments intended to be worn for the ringing in of the New Year. There were silver and gold sequined dresses with rhinestone-studded spaghetti straps, complete with fur-lined velvet capes. And as I stood gawking at the evening wear in front of me, I had but a single thought: "What are these people thinking?!"

Does anyone know anyone who is actually going somewhere on New Year's Eve who would have an opportunity to wear an evening gown—with or without sequins?

My guess is, most of us are spending the dawn of the New Year like we spend most of our evenings. And for many of us that means with our kids. Now, maybe this is because the going rate for a sitter for this yearly event would supposedly necessitate our having to take out a second mortgage. But I suspect it is more likely because that is where we choose to be.

Personally, my family and I will be attending a party at a friend's house to usher in the big event. Don't get me wrong though. I am not saying there won't be a lot of the traditional New Year's hoopla going on.

Glitter. Yes, there will be lots of glitter. No, most of it will not come from sequins on the dresses of the women there. Most of the glitter will come from tubes and be from the kids' crafts that will be going on in the basement. So, technically, our night will be filled with glitter. True, some of it will even end up on our clothes as well.

Drinking. There will be a lot of drinking, too. The juice will be absolutely flowing. Some will be red. Some will be white. Most of it will be in a container called a juice box.

Dancing. Yes, there will be dancing at the New Year's Eve celebration, too. Most of it will be my kids dancing outside the bathroom while having to wait their turn to go. This will be a direct result of the free-flowing juice mentioned before.

Fine dining. All of us parents in attendance will agree that it is, indeed, a fine dining experience, if nothing is stained in the hostess's house the entire night. Actually each of us parents will think it is a fine dining experience even if something is spilled, as long as it is not our child who spilled it.

Romance. Yes, when the stroke of midnight falls and I am ready to greet the coming year held tightly in the arms of my husband, there will most likely be a child or two in our arms as well. The first kisses I receive in the new year will probably leave chocolate stains on my cheek. But somehow, the whole thing will leave me with a feeling that the night was a success. For a new year dawning definitely teaches me something and it has nothing to do with what shoes to wear with a fur-lined velvet cape. No, the new year simply reminds me that the years are flying by a little too quickly. There should be many years ahead that could offer the opportunity for wining, dining and dancing.

But for now, we choose to embrace the sweetness of the simple things.

Like glitter from a tube and juice from a box.

And a chocolate kiss at midnight.

CHAPTER SEVEN:
The Learning Heart

. . . for wisdom will come into your heart, and knowledge
will be pleasant to your soul.
—Proverbs 2:10

SPRING BREAK

We had agreed. There would be no Florida vacation this spring
break.

With my mom and dad spending the cold month of March down
in sunny Florida, and their gracious invitation to join them for
a few days, if we so desired, it was, indeed, very hard not to
desire it. But our school district's April spring break and proficiency testing helped us realize this was the time we had to
play grown-up, stay up North and put another log on the fire.

But then it happened.

The chain of events of the last week in March made it geneti-
cally impossible for my husband to adhere to our playing
grown-up decision.

The Ohio State Buckeye basketball team made it to the final

four play-offs in, of all places, Florida.

And the final testosterone-induced deciding factor was: we got tickets to the games.

But we still had the original dilemma of that April spring break and those proficiency tests to consider. With this in mind, we did what any loving parents of four children would do.

We went without the kids.

With the other set of grandparents innocently agreeing to hold down the fort for us, we had one day to prepare for our southern migration. And, because my fort has never been accused of being overly clean, there was some major work to do. Instead of spending this time packing, I, of course, spent it hosing out my refrigerator and scraping heaven knows what off my kitchen floor.

Then there were the little extra things I felt compelled to do to make my absence easier to bear for the kids. Buying and wrapping a small gift for each child for every day we were gone made me realize we had a lot of children. And for the younger ones, so they could visualize when we would be back, I put pictures on their beds, writing on each one how many days of the vacation were left. Then I taped these timekeepers to each of their beds, informing them that when they took off the last picture we would be home on that very day. Of course, my youngest called me on the second day of the trip and informed me he had ripped them all off his bed that day and expected me to uphold my promise and be home any minute.

Nevertheless, we did migrate south, enjoying the beach, the freedom and, oh yeah, the game.

Then the thing that ruins every vacation happened.

It was time to go home.

Suddenly, the fifteen-hour drive straight through the night that made us feel like young, hip college students on the way down made us feel like old, tired parents on the way home.

Because it was my birthday, we had wanted to arrive home early to spend the day with the kids. We ended up waking them at 6:30 A.M. By 6:45 A.M., I was ready to go back to Florida but I would have settled for going to bed. Of course, that was not in the parental cards of the day.

I was back to reality and I thought I was doing a good job of covering up my exhaustion caused by not sleeping the night before. But I found out I was wrong.

Perhaps it was the dramatic way I was resting my head on the bathtub while giving my youngest his bath. Maybe it was the deep sighs I injected into every conversation. Whatever it was, my other little boy picked up on it too quickly. Before he went to bed that night, he handed me an envelope and said, "Happy birthday, Mommy." As I opened it, I was shocked to find his entire life savings, which amounted to roughly eight dollars and some odd cents. I sincerely thanked him, but assured him I did not need his money. With this, his eyes began to water and his little lip began to tremble. Finally, the dam of tears burst, as he cried, "But, Mommy, it is your birthday and I just want you to be happy, but you seem so sad!"

Of course, my own guilty but tired tears soon ungracefully mixed with his, as I tried to explain the difference between sleepy and sad. Somehow, though, as I held him in my arms that night, I felt absolutely refreshed.

And, I realized something interesting.

I knew all along a Florida vacation could not guarantee you happiness.

And I had always told my kids, money could not buy it.

But somehow, my son had done just that.

He had bought happiness for me.

For roughly eight dollars and some odd cents.

The

Book

of

Mom

Snow Freedom

It was the first big snowfall of the year, and I had looked forward to this moment for a long time. It wasn't the snow I had been anxiously anticipating. No, what I had been waiting for is the day my kids would be able to frolic in the fallen snow without me being beside them in the cold, ready to retrieve a stuck boot out of a snowdrift or to comfort a toddler who had fallen face down in the frigid flakes.

Now it wasn't that I didn't enjoy the crunch of snow under my own boots. It was simply the fact that snow is, well, cold. And I am partial to circulation in my fingertips and toes. Not to mention what a knit hat does to my hair.

But I didn't have to worry about that any more. The days of frostbite and bad hat-hair were behind me now. With my youngest finally old enough to stay upright in the snow, I knew he could frolic with the best of them while I would be able to sip that hot cup of coffee while watching from my very warm chair by the window.

And so I began to bundle up my children for that adult-free frolic in the snow. This endeavor led me to dream yet another dream. This dream would be for the day when all my kids had a pair of mittens that actually matched for two days in a row. But, then again, I know some dreams are simply too impossible to come true.

What Parents Know by Heart

Finally, they all plodded out the door clothed in enough winter wear to have survived a trek through the Himalayas. All, that is, except my oldest. She thought it was too cold to venture outside. Besides, she added, the hat I had picked out for her would ruin her hair. Where do kids get these ideas?

And so I sat down with my hot cup of coffee to watch from my chair by the window. I saw the unsuccessful attempts to make a snowman result in a snowball fight full of giggles. I watched as they tried to catch falling flakes on their tongues. I observed my little ones lying on their backs on top of the freshly fallen snow, methodically waving their arms and legs up and down in an effort to make their very own snow angels.

My chair was nice and warm, but somehow, I suddenly felt a chill. No one had opened the door, though. It was just that I had finally opened my eyes. The chill had come from a cold realization. I guess I realized I really didn't want simply to watch my kids from my window. I really didn't want to watch life from my window. I wanted to experience life: frostbite, bad hair and all. By the end of that day, my backyard was covered in snow angels. Some of them were, indeed, adult size, too.

And that night as I reflected on these backyard angels I understood how soon they would be melting out of my yard and my house.

There may come a day when I will have to watch the world from my window. But until then, I want people to meet me and know I am living life, not just watching it. I hope they will be able to say that about me.

Right after they stop laughing at my hair.

VACATION DESTINATION

We made it.

That is to say that we made sixteen hours in a car driving through the night to make it to a Florida vacation destination. Did I mention there were six of us packed into the minivan? And did I mention that the adults were outnumbered two to four by the kids?

We left Cincinnati at seven in the evening. We got a later start than usual due to my oldest child's activities that we, of course, had to work around. The delay was good for me though. I spent the day doing all the mommy chores like arranging the things we would need on the way down. Earlier that afternoon I received the call from the man who was repairing my broken TV that plugs into the car. At least that is what I had hoped he was doing. He, though, informed me that the TV was beyond repair. A feeling of panic shot through me. I had been banking on the ease of plugging in the TV and watching a marathon of Disney videos until we hit the Florida line. But with that not being the case, I had only a couple of hours to build up our supplies of car games, snacks, music, crafts and books.

One hour before we were to set out, I was taking inventory. I was pleased with my selection of items that would amuse the kids on our way to Florida. But my pat on the back was ended with another feeling of panic.

I realized I had forgotten to pack.

Yes, in all my great organization of activities, I had forgotten to pack our suitcases.

Luckily, a wardrobe for the beach doesn't need to consist of much more than a swimsuit and a sweatshirt. Someone forgot

115

What
Parents
Know
by
Heart

to tell my teenager that, though. Simply for starters she packed four pairs of shoes.

Somewhere in the hustle and bustle of all this, my youngest daughter asked, "Mommy, aren't you excited?"

It might be worth noting that at this point I had perhaps gotten a little overly anxious. My head was pounding and the children were all squealing with excitement. I decided to lie down for just a minute. Of course, I should point out that I decided to lie down right in the middle of the kitchen floor.

"Mommy," my daughter repeated, "aren't you excited?" as she waved suntan lotion under my nose as if it were actually smelling salts.

Through my clenched teeth, I managed to say, "I will be excited once we get there."

She persisted, "Aren't you excited about the ride, though?"

I shut my eyes and thought of the upcoming ride through the night with four kids, no sleep and no television for support. I repeated, "I will be excited when we get there."

"But, Mommy," my wise daughter, by now rubbing suntan lotion on my arm, observed, "we'll all be together. And that makes getting there half the fun."

Maybe it was the smell of coconut oil. Maybe it was the cold hardwood floor against my back. But whatever it was, I was feeling better.

And I realized my daughter was right.

We spend so much time waiting and worrying about reaching our destination that we sometimes forget that getting there is, indeed, half the fun. When all is said and done in this journey of life, it won't matter how many miles it took us to reach our destination, what we packed or how quickly we arrived. The only thing that will matter is to be able to say that we were with the people we wanted to be with while on this journey to our destination.

Only then will we truly be able to say, "We made it."

With or without a TV.

BAT AND BALL

I just don't have "it."

That thing inside you that makes you actually look forward to sporting events has never been spotted in my genetic make-up. I know it's not a gender thing—many of my female friends actually enjoy sports. I simply have come to realize that I just wasn't cut out to be an athletic supporter.

Unless, of course, I have actually given birth to one of the players on the sport team. If that is the case, I can be found court-side, field-side or pool-side as enthusiastic as the best of them. But any other time, I would rather not go.

Now, living in Cincinnati, this personality trait of mine can be seen as somewhat unpatriotic. I confess—I know very little about our very own hometown Reds. And since, as far as I know, I have not given birth to any of the ballplayers, I really have little desire to go to a game.

And so it was that I was not present the other night when my two sons went to their first Reds game this year accompanied by their daddy and their grandpa.

My eight-year-old took with him to this game a ball glove and a determination that he was going to catch a ball. My five-year-old simply took with him the desire to bring home something that was at least as good, if not better, than whatever it was that his older brother was planning to bring home.

I am told the game went on and on. The threat of rain, accompanied by the odds against the home team winning, made several people leave early. My eight-year-old persisted in his quest for a ball. He soon moved down to some empty seats that were available right above the dugout. My somewhat shy five-year-old decided to stay with his daddy and grandpa, as he intently kept a keen eye on his brother's progress. Quickly my older son made some new friends in a group of compassionate men who took his mission upon themselves.

"Hey!" they yelled to the dugout below, as they lifted my son up to be seen. "How about throwing this kid a ball?" I suspected they all were remembering a time in their lives when they were little and thought that catching a major league ball was better than any amount of money imaginable. I also guessed that whatever "it" was that I am lacking in the sports gene category, they, indeed, had in abundance.

The ball quest went on for only a short while before my triumphant son emerged from the crowd with the coveted ball and a smile that lit the stands.

Carefully carrying this prized possession cupped gently in his eight-year-old hands, as if the ball were made of glass, he valiantly returned to his incredulous family. He only had to show his little brother his conquest before his little brother had overcome his shyness enough to run down to meet and greet his older brother's new best friends.

At this point, my husband and father-in-law knew that the chances of each of the boys getting a ball on this night would be slim at best. But the good-hearted fans who so successfully helped my older son catch his first ball, were up for the challenge with the younger one, as well.

"Hey!" they began their chants at the dugout again. "How about something for this little guy, too?"

And then, to the total disbelief of my husband, father-in-law and older son, my five-year-old emerged from the huddle carrying,

119

What
Parents
Know
by
Heart

not a major league ball, but a major league bat. And as he proudly carried his bat in a manner that brought to mind the carrying of the Olympic torch, the crowd around them began to cheer for him.

But I suspect they were also cheering for that certain something that they all remember from their own childhood.

They were remembering why they love the game. They were rediscovering what "it" is.

And now there are two little boys at my house who have a treasure that will last a lifetime.

And they also have a ball and a bat.

Cool Mom

I wanted to be the cool mom.

When I held my first child for the first time, I remember thinking of all the things we would do together. I thought of all the fun times, the giggles and the shared secrets. I wanted her to think I was the coolest mom in the world. I wanted to be her best friend.

Flash forward thirteen years and I have come to the realization that the cool mom might make the grade on television sitcoms, but, in reality, she flunks the parental challenge.

Take the other weekend, for example. Please.

My thirteen-year-old had been planning an outing at a local pizza place for well over a week. The day before the anticipated outing, she went to a friend's house after school. But, she forgot to call home to let me know this change of plans—for thirty minutes. Now, anyone who has kids knows what scenarios you can conjure up in your imagination in thirty minutes. By the time she called, I was annoyed but I let it slide, most likely due to that coolness quota that I had been striving for.

To make a long story short, the afternoon adventures did not end there. My daughter forgot to call one more time in the course of the day.

Suddenly, I was a little too hot to even try to be cool.

I informed my daughter that she was grounded for the rest of the weekend, due to her forgetfulness. She seemed accepting of this punishment until she remembered the pizza outing that had been planned for a week.

She begged.

She pleaded.

What
Parents
Know
by
Heart

She cried.

I have to say that this was one of the hardest decisions I have had to make as a parent. It broke my heart to see the tears of my child—a child who never causes much fuss. It would have been so easy to give in, to be the cool mom. But I held firm.

The next day, one of my daughter's friends even called to beg me to go lenient on her since it was her first offense. Her motion for leniency was denied. What the well-meaning friend didn't realize was that, if I could withstand the tears of my daughter, I could withstand anything.

And what neither of them realized was that yesterday's word *cool* had been replaced by today's word *responsibility.*

Lately, I've been noticing a trend in signs. My grocery store has a sign that says it is not responsible for damage done by their carts. My dry cleaners has a sign that states it's not responsible for stains. The play yard that asks for kids to take off their shoes to play has a sign declaring they are not responsible for any shoes being stolen. When I sign my kids up for any sport or field trip, there is always a place for me to sign that says I understand that the sponsoring party is not responsible for anything at all that might happen to my child.

Maybe that should be our new national motto: "We're not responsible."

But, as parents, we can't say that about our children. We can't hang a sign around their neck that says we are not responsible for how they turn out. We are responsible. And we owe it to our kids to teach them how to be responsible.

It's a scary world out there. The traditional threats of drugs and drinking are now amplified with the intensity of Internet interactions. A child now has even more chances to make life-changing decisions.

Giggles and shared secrets are great, but for pure survival, we cannot forget to teach our children responsibility.

Granted, responsibility is not very high on the coolness list, but I think I have finally come to an overdue realization.

Our children are most likely to have hundreds of friends in their lives.

Still, the basic fact remains, they have only two parents.

Indeed, that is an incredible responsibility.

But it's actually pretty cool.

CHAPTER EIGHT:
The Seeking Heart

*From there you will seek the Lord your
God and you will find him if you search
after him with all your heart and soul.*
—Deuteronomy 4:29

SCRIPT OF LIFE

Have you ever watched a movie and cynically doubted how certain events ever could plausibly have happened as they were scripted?

I have discovered that sometimes the big script of life throws us even more unbelievable ironies that force us to stop and pay attention for at least a little while.

This thought was ever in my mind while I was sitting in a chapel at Christ Hospital saying a prayer for two people who both happened to be patients there. The irony of the fact that they would both be at that hospital at that very time overwhelms me still.

The first patient who was the recipient of my prayer intention was my sister-in-law. She was in labor on the ninth floor of the hospital, waiting to deliver her first baby.

And while I was praying for a safe delivery, I had to realize that the fact that my sister-in-law was in labor at all was already an incredible answer to a prayer.

You see, the news of her pregnancy ended her painful five-year ordeal with infertility. Over those years, all in the family shared in her heartache as much as we could. But there were certain depths of the hurt no one could fully understand.

No one except her husband.

For it was her husband, my brother-in-law, who had fought cancer seven years earlier and had won. The treatment for his cancer had blessedly cured the cancer, but what had ended the cancer battle had begun the infertility battle.

Together, they weathered many doctor visits.

Together they weathered high hopes being repeatedly dashed.

Together they weathered the storms that come to those whose hearts are so full, but whose arms are so empty.

Then, the miracle happened. As if, indeed, scripted by Hollywood, my sister-in-law and brother-in-law, together, announced they were expecting—on Mother's Day last year.

And so I sat in the chapel of Christ Hospital praying for a miracle baby I had never met, but already dearly loved.

But coincidentally enough, at that very moment, I was also praying for yet another patient at Christ Hospital. For at that very second, a dear friend of mine was on the sixth floor undergoing surgery to repair damage done to his hip by the ravages of cancer.

And as I sat in the chapel praying for my two requests, I could not help but be touched by the irony of it all.

On the ninth floor were two parents who were waiting to hold their miracle for which they had been waiting for years. They were waiting and praying to bring their son into this world.

And on the sixth floor, there waited two parents who were also waiting for a miracle. They were waiting and praying to keep their son in this world.

In the big script of life we never know what ironies will touch us along the way. Some will bring a laugh of complete joy. Others will bring a tear of utter sorrow.

So many times we wish we could simply flip ahead in the script to see what scenes are coming.

But we know we can't.

All we can do is take a deep breath.

Turn one page at a time.

And pray.

127

THE DANCE

"I double-dog dare you to throw the ball with me when we get home," my youngest son challenged his older brother from the back seat of my van.

"That's not how you use a double-dog dare," my much more worldly older boy explained to his sibling. "You use a double-dog dare when you really, really want someone to do something, but you don't think they have enough nerve to do it."

Eavesdropping on their innocent conversation made me think of the not-so-innocent conversation I had had with my oldest child the night before. You see, she was telling me about a recent social dance some of her friends had gone to. It was their first event since becoming high school students. Now, while it, indeed, seems like a lifetime ago, I do remember being in high school. And while it, too, seems like a lifetime ago, I also remember teaching high school a little more than a decade ago. But still, I was not prepared for what they reported. And, what is worse, these students were not prepared for it either.

I guess many students in attendance came to the dance in a less than sober state of mind and body. My daughter's friends were embarrassed for the upperclassmen who had to hit the bottle before hitting the dance floor. It was bad enough that the cigarettes that were being passed around burned their eyes, but what really burned a memory in their freshman minds was the drunken behavior of people they looked up to.

Suddenly I realized that the days of innocent double-dog dares were over for my oldest and her friends. From this moment on, the dares they would face in life could become life altering. Decisions from now on no longer had the luxury of being made with "eeny meeny miney moe." And the wrong decisions they might make would no longer be made better by their mothers simply kissing a boo-boo.

And all this seemed to happen overnight.

I understand that you can tell me I am being naive if I expect this behavior doesn't rear its ugly little head until college. You can tell me that this is simply what happens with high school aged children these days. But I disagree. And it is the very word *children* that makes me disagree. Isn't the legal drinking age twenty-one these days? Don't you have to be eighteen to purchase cigarettes? How many of the intoxicated upperclassmen drove themselves to the dance? That in and of itself is an accident waiting to happen, in many more ways than one. I have to wonder what we are waiting for.

We are robbing our kids of their innocence by allowing this behavior to exist under the label: "That's just what happens in high school." Have we lowered the bar of expectations so low now that kids can step—or stumble—across it without giving it a second thought?

What Parents Know by Heart

It needs to be said that many other kids there that night were not happy with the behavior of some of the older students. And they were not pressured to do anything they didn't want to do. But this was the first social dance of their high school life. How long will it be before this behavior is not only accepted but embraced as the norm? After all, it is high school, you know.

I do know that we cannot change what is happening in all high schools around the world these days. But I suspect we can make a difference, one school at a time, one child at a time.

We can start with our own children and grandchildren, nieces and nephews. We can raise the bar of expectations for them. We can let them know that once their innocence is gone, they can never get it back. They deserve better.

I'm willing to try.

Are you?

I dare you. No—I double-dog dare you.

The

Book

of

Mom

9/11

When I am upset, I tend to clean my house.

My husband might say that from the looks of things, I don't get upset very often.

But I had plenty of opportunity to clean on Tuesday, 9/11—or as it will forever be remembered: Tuesday, 9-1-1.

I had just gone upstairs at 9:45 A.M. to check on my oldest, who was home from school because she was sick to her stomach. What we were about to hear would make us all sick.

My husband called from work. "Are you watching TV?" When I said that I wasn't, he immediately said, "Turn on the television." Somehow I knew I didn't have to ask what channel.

Who could believe it? Two planes had crashed into the World Trade Center in New York City. There was a rumor about the Pentagon. As I watched with the phone to my ear, I began to tremble. I felt numb with shock. "Keep watching," my husband advised.

131

What

Parents

Know

by

Heart

But I couldn't. In the face of such destruction, I had to do something constructive. So I mowed the grass.

When I came in, I heard about the twin towers crumbling to the ground. I saw something flying. But soon I realized that the forms I saw were not flying, but falling—to their deaths. They were people. Moms, dads, brothers, sisters. People.

The screen filled with screaming, frantically running people as they raced a fireball explosion, understanding that it truly was a matter of life and death. I kept reminding myself that this was not incredible special effects of a Hollywood movie. As unreal as it seemed, it was, indeed, real.

It was then I had to vacuum the house.

Soon it was confirmed that the Pentagon was, in fact, a target of one of the crashes. Then, it was corroborated that a site close to Camp David was also involved in one. Then, the word *highjacked* kept coming up in all the reports. Terrorists infiltrating four planes on two different airlines. And the two airlines were, of course, named United and American.

Reporters shoved cameras in any face they could see. Most of those faces were stained with soot and tears, if not blood.

I had to call the elementary school where my two youngest attend. I suspected the older kids would be told what was going on in this world, but I had hoped that the younger ones would remain in the blissful dark for as long a possible—or at least until they could hear the news from their parents.

I talked to the school secretary who said, "Don't worry. We are right now living in a safe little bubble."

I asked if I could live there, too.

But instead, I changed the bed sheets.

And this was a good idea, because later that night, after the kids found out and were attempting to get to sleep, they had too many questions for the nighttime routine to happen as usual. For that reason, the youngest three all ended up in bed with my husband and me that night. The bed was quite full, but so, too, were all our hearts.

And as I lay in bed hearing my children's peaceful breathing next to me, I tried in vain to get my own breathing to match theirs. But it was not easy.

I tried to focus on the good and not the evil. I tried to think of the rescue workers, blood donations, the president quoting the Bible on television, people slowing down, listening to each other, saying "I love you" more. But still I fought the urge to get up and clean something.

But in the end I did the only thing that truly cleanses away the filth of the world on a day like that. I prayed. For that is where the healing truly starts.

Pray. Pray for the victims. Pray for the survivors. Pray for the rescue workers and politicians. Pray for the children shown in the foreign news clips who were gleefully dancing in the street upon hearing of the American tragedy. And yes, pray for the terrorists who caused all this. Pray to whomever or whatever you hold sacred in your faith. And if you have no faith to believe in, that's your right. It is, after all a free country.

And I will pray that it stays that way.

What
Parents
Know
by
Heart

REAL LIFE BOMB

"What does a bomb look like in real life?"

This honest and innocent question came from my little boy upon hearing that the United States had just dropped a bomb on Afghanistan.

I was at a soccer game. I was actually just thinking how—for the first time in three weeks—things felt like they were getting back to normal. The girls were putting all their energies into playing soccer. The parents were putting all their energies into yelling advice at both the players and the referees. My two younger boys were tossing a football during the game. It was so simple. It was so normal.

This is when I allowed myself to have a brief moment of hope. No more than five minutes later did my husband arrive.

"It's begun," he announced. "The U.S. started bombing Afghanistan."

As we were discussing this military maneuver, my youngest child came up to us. This is when he asked his question, "What does a bomb look like in real life?"

And I realized I didn't know.

Aside from movies I have seen, I never had any reason to learn what a bomb looks like. I just didn't know.

But there are a lot of things I realize I don't know now.

I don't know what a Tomahawk cruise missile looks like. I don't know what a village in Afghanistan looks like. I don't even know that I can point out Afghanistan on a map. I even had to look up how to spell it before I could type it.

What is more, I don't know what the answer to all this is.

And even though I don't like it, I understand that something had to be done. A lot of people are scared.

I just took a trip by airplane. I confess I was anxious. The airports were moving, functioning and going about their business. But there was an incredibly eerie silence amid the hundreds of people coming and going. And there was distrust. You could see it in the eyes of those you met. Everyone was checking out everyone else. No one was to be trusted. We waited an hour to pass through security at one of the airports. But I was grateful for the caution they were showing. And I have to admit I was grateful to be blonde.

"What does a bomb look like in real life?"

I have no idea. I am still just trying to get over the fact that my children are in a position to have to worry about what bombs and terrorists and war look like. It's somewhat ironic. For years I have tried so hard to keep the movies and television shows that my children watch to be age appropriate so as not to give them nightmares about the make-believe evils of the world. And now the news has become the most frightening thing my kids can see on television. True evil is so much more frightening than make-believe.

But somehow we go on. We go to work. We go to school. And of course, there are always those soccer games.

We blanket ourselves in our flag and our faith, seeing them both as sources of comfort like we have never known before. And we pray.

We pray for the wisdom needed to guide the world's leaders. We pray for ice-cold hearts to melt. We pray for peace that we once took so for granted.

And we pray that our children will never truly find out what a bomb looks like in real life.

*What
Parents
Know
by
Heart*

The Bake Sale

These days everyone is looking for a little hope. A way of making a difference.

Even the kids are feeling this way. When President Bush suggested that every child in America should each earn a dollar and send it to the White House where it would be sent on to the starving Afghan children, many felt it was a chance to finally see some good news.

And it was.

My middle daughter's class discussed this and set up a fund at their school. Each child was given the mission of raising that dollar. My daughter came home ready to work. Now this is the child of mine who always takes life one step further. If everyone else is giggling—this child will guffaw. If others' eyes are brimming with tears—she will cry buckets. If everyone else is earning a dollar—she knows what she wants to do.

"I want to bake cookies and brownies . . . I want to make lemonade . . . I want to have a stand on Saturday and all the money I raise can go to the children in Afghanistan," she excitedly informed me without pausing for a breath.

Willing to help, but feeling way too tired to take on one of my daughter's dramatic undertakings, I made an alternate suggestion: "Why don't you just rake the leaves and the money you earn can go to the children?"

But my eager entrepreneur would not waver. Saturday arrived and with the help of a friend, she started working diligently on her signs. "Help the Children of Afghanistan," one said. "Kids helping kids," said another. "Kool-Aid—25 cents a cup." After more than an hour spent working on these pieces of art, I did make the observation to my daughter and her friend that it would be hard to have a bake sale without baking anything.

After praising me on my business knowledge, the girls began baking brownies and making Kool-Aid. By three o'clock in the afternoon, the girls were ready to go with the little picnic table in the driveway—complete with the American flag in the background. Soon the whole family got involved in the running of the show. My oldest did more signs. One son tried to drum up business by riding around the neighborhood on his bike bursting out in patriotic songs anytime anyone would listen. And my youngest son got to hold the cash box.

And it wasn't long before that cash box started bulging. For three hours people stopped by the little picnic table with the American flag nearby and they reached into their hearts as well as their pockets. Many didn't even take the nourishment that was for sale. But I know from their gentle smiles and their reassuring nods that they appreciated the subtle nourishment they received simply by stopping. The mail delivery person, police officer, neighbor, stranger—they all stopped by to try to help a few kids who were trying to help a few kids.

It was heartwarming for me to watch. I was so glad my daughter persisted and didn't take me up on my offer to have her rake the leaves instead. The spirit of the day was something she will remember for a long time. Much older kids like me, will remember it even longer.

By the end of the day, they had collected more than seventy dollars to send to the children's fund. In her pride and excitement, my daughter's feet could barely touch the ground. She felt as if she had single-handedly discovered the key to a better world.

What
Parents
Know
by
Heart

And just maybe she was right.

After all, everyone is looking for a little hope these days. And that Saturday it could be found in my driveway.

For twenty-five cents a cup.

The

Book

of

Mom

CHAPTER NINE:
The Grateful Heart

I will give thanks to the Lord with my whole
heart; I will tell of all your wonderful deeds.
—Psalm 9:1

THE TRIP

There are four simple words in the English language that I
believe could have been used in the primitive torture chambers.
At the least, these words must have been around for generations. I believe as far back as the pioneers who would load their
loved ones into their horse-drawn buggies and head across the
prairie, parents must have bristled at these words.

"Are we there yet?"

I even suspect that during the caveman times, before language
was even developed, the father caveman would be taking his
cave son on a hunting and gathering excursion. And before the
parental unit had even wondered far from the cave, the overly
anxious son would grunt in such a way that the cave father
would know he was bugging him with a not yet invented

phrase, as follows:

"Are we there yet?"

It would not be as bothersome if this were truthfully an innocent question asked with the sole purpose of obtaining an answer about one's destination. But instead, I believe it is an actual overt attempt by our children to drive us parents over the proverbial brink.

"Are we there yet?"

Thus began our ten-hour drive to Michigan for our family vacation. I wouldn't have minded this first inquiry so much, except for that fact that we actually hadn't even started the car.

"Are we there yet?"

The next time this was asked, we were stopping for the first of our five bathroom breaks. Of course, each potty break coincided with refueling, not just for the car, but for the kids as well. This did strike me as a vicious cycle we were perpetuating.

"Are we there yet?"

This time the question was asked while my own body was twisted in such a way across the backseats of my van that I wasn't even sure where each limb had landed. No, we had not had an accident. I was just breaking my own mandatory seatbelt rule in order to fetch something that had fallen for one of my children. However, I did have my standards. This rule was only broken to obtain something incredibly important, like a piece of gum.

"Are we there yet?"

At this moment I was interrupted from my role of judge, trying to decide which child had touched or breathed on which other child. This job was made all the more difficult as the testimony simply consisted of a repetition of "did not . . . did, too."

Then it happened. There was one precious moment when all were quiet in the backseats. Miraculously, all four kids had fallen asleep at the same time. And as I took a moment to look back at my van cluttered with enough debris to have kept us on the road for ten days instead of hours, I couldn't help but notice the looks on the sleeping faces. Each face possessed an expression of such sweet excitement and pure anticipation as they dreamt of their impending vacation destination. At last, I understood something that I had forgotten on this journey.

This was it. No need to keep waiting.

"Are we there yet?"

In so many ways, we were.

What

Parents

Know

by

Heart

THE PLAY

Someone once said, "All the world's a stage and most of us are simply stagehands."

Well, recently, I was a stagemom.

You see, my oldest was in a play at her school.

Now, I have never been a believer in pushing my kids. In fact, I often go to the other extreme. At times, I can be heard saying these less than encouraging words: "Oh, I'm sure you don't want to play soccer [be on the swim team] [try out for the play], do you?"

I say this not for lack of faith in my children, but simply for lack of energy in me. Because I know that the more things my kids are involved in, the more things I consequently will be involved in. But in spite of my lack of pushing, my kids have gotten overly involved in everything.

So when my oldest came home and announced she was going to try out for the fall musical, I may not have been the most enthusiastic mother.

And when she told me she got a part in the play, my excitement for her was held in check with the realization of the commitment that had to be made by the actors and the actors' families. There were rehearsals to attend, little jobs to volunteer for and costumes to make. And this didn't even take into account the time spent helping to learn lines and songs and dance numbers. Now we were already shuffling schedules around for soccer games, cheerleading practices and swimming. And does anyone remember that thing called homework? At the rate we were going, we would be lucky to all sit down for dinner together sometime next February.

So I admit, I was not the biggest dramatic supporter of the play.

But then it was opening night.

The curtain opened.

And the lights went up.

Suddenly sitting there in the auditorium filled with my family and the families of all the other little middle school thespians, my heart began to race. As the first scene began and the children sang, danced and acted their hearts out, I was filled with such pride watching my child and all the others demonstrate what all the shuffling of time and sacrificing of dinners had been for. I think there is very little that can compare to the feeling parents have when they are watching their children do something they are good at, enjoy and are learning from all at the same time.

And as I sat watching the last scene with tears in my eyes, I couldn't help but marvel at how fast children grow up. For now I was watching these young teens who were now confidently saying their lines to a packed theater, but I was remembering them as a group of little eight-year-olds who once put on mini song-and-dance routines in my backyard.

I guess the world really is a stage. And right now I am feeling very grateful for my role of mom in this busy play we call life. Every day is a new scene. No one is exactly like the other. Sometimes I am sure of my lines. And other times I stammer for something to say. But no matter how chaotic the play gets with all the scene changes and shifts in characters, I want to try to remember to applaud the wonder of this precious production.

The worst thing that could happen is to not appreciate the play until the curtain closes.

Mom

I've heard it said that all great writers must have had childhoods full of some degree of difficulty and sad memories.

If that is the case, it is going to be mainly one person's fault that I will not go down in history as a great writer. And that person would, of course, be my mother.

Reflecting on my childhood, I strain to find that unique upbringing that some writers expand upon to find their particular voice in the literary world.

Traveling down that memory lane, I could say that while growing up we were so poor my mom had to sew our clothing. But the truth was she just liked to make us special outfits from time to time. And the fact that she would be up until 2:00 A.M. the night before Easter because she was hand-smocking a dress I was to wear to church the next day really doesn't make for great tales of childhood woe. So, thanks to my mom, I will never write that great American novel about growing up dressed in rags.

I guess I could say that sometimes she would blindfold us children and purposefully scare us with bizarre things such as low-hanging crepe paper in the neighbor's garage. But the truth is that she did that on Halloween to entertain the neighborhood kids. And annual fun-filled parties just don't tug at the old heartstrings at all. So, thanks to my mom, I will never write that award-winning essay about an apathetic mother, either.

Maybe I could say she eccentrically used to make beds out of tissue boxes and toilets out of bleach bottles. But, again, the truth to that would be that she, indeed, did make the home furnishings out of odds and ends, but the home she was furnishing was my Barbie doll's house. And a mom who plays with her kids and helps them to be creative is just not what is selling these days. Therefore, thanks to my mom, there goes my chance at an Academy Award for my screen play based on an eccentric mother.

It's possible that I could stir up some interest in my childhood if I mention that there is a certain smell that I smell even today that still reminds me of my mother. Of course, the fact that it is Jergen's hand lotion, due to the fact that she put it on every night before kissing us good night, takes away any sort of edge the idea might have offered. So, thanks to my mom, I won't even be able to stretch that one into a short story of any interest at all.

Perhaps I could say that shortly after I left home, my mom's heart was filled with new children whom she loved in a new and deeper way than she had ever known before. There is no doubt in my mind that she would move both heaven and earth for these new children. Of course, the truth to that matter is that those adored new children are my children. And what does the world need to hear about a woman who dotes upon her grandchildren? So, thanks to my mom, there will be no Broadway musical coming from me about an emotionally fickle mom.

There you have it. No pain, no suffering, no angst. Nothing of the things that mold and create a brilliant writer.

And looking back, there is only one thing left that I can say with total honesty.

Thanks . . . to my mom.

SUMMER GAMES

I learned something today from two little teachers who have never even been to primary school. And the classroom didn't have a chalkboard. But it did have an inflatable pool. It was my backyard.

You see, I was watching two four-year-olds do what they were meant to do on a hot summer day: play, play, play.

My son had invited his young friend over to play in his little pool. Under the guise of lifeguarding this two-foot-deep area of water, I did what I have not been doing much of this summer: sit, sit, sit.

The summer has been going strong with activities. One daughter had 7:30 A.M. swim team practice. My other daughter had 9:00 A.M. practice. The boys had swimming lessons at 11:00 and 11:30. Pepper into this schedule swim meets and various camps and you can see why the only time I caught myself sitting at all was when I was behind the wheel of my car.

I felt like I was no longer experiencing things in my life as much as I was simply checking them off my to-do list.

That's when my four-year-old swimmers taught me something. I cannot watch little children play together without marveling at how natural the whole process is. As an adult, I am often tempted to offer suggestions, rules and games to play for any given moment. But kids teach us they don't always want or, more importantly, need that structure we so strive for as grown-ups. In fact, they blossom most when they are simply left to play, play, play.

Immediately upon hitting the water, my son and his friend began to interact with each other totally on their own terms. They delighted in the fact that they were completely making up the rules as they went along.

"Let's run three times around the pool and then jump in," one would giggle as he began to run, followed happily by his friend.

"Now, let's fall into the water, but you can't get your head wet at all," the other one chimed in.

"Let's swing on the swings four times and then run to the pool and fall on our bellies!"

After several minutes of their own version of follow-the-leader they began the preschool diving division of the afternoon.

"Hey," one would holler, "do you know what this dive is called?" Contorting his body into a shape I cannot do justice to with mere words, he jumped into the water as he announced, "It's called the rhino-pencil dive"

"This one's called the cloud bomb!"

"This one's the dragon dive!"

"Watch my doggie dip dive!"

All the while they were playing there was never a shortage of that most precious sound, which I believe has the power to heal: giggling.

And as I watched them play their made-up games, I felt a warmth come over me that wasn't due to the fact that I had forgotten my sunscreen. No, this warmth was the dawning of an appreciation for this game of life that begs for you to come and play, play, play.

And that's when I learned something.

I learned I want to try to stop simply checking my days off my to-do list so that I might thoroughly enjoy this game.

Maybe I'll make up some rules as I go along.

Who knows? I might even start to giggle.

THE BALL

I had a date the other night.

There was music and dancing and flowers and beanbag tossing. My date picked out what I would wear. He had a particular preference for the sparkly necklace over the one I usually wear around my neck. He had been looking forward to our date all day. He even took a nap in preparation for it.

You see, my son's preschool just completed a unit on fairy tales. After a couple of weeks of talking about kings and queens and castles, it was announced that they would sponsor a ball. All of the children were encouraged to come in whatever regal attire they desired. Each child was to invite one parent to accompany them to the ball.

My young kingly escort was dressed in a royal blue blazer. Topping off his ensemble, was a white fake fur coat purchased at a garage sale ten years earlier. That purchase has more than paid for itself as all my kids have worn it at one time or another for various Halloween costumes, from that of fairy princess to Elvis.

And that night it kept my noble date warm.

As the youngest of four, I suppose it is more normal for my little one to simply be along for the ride. Rarely are activities solely about him. But that night was, indeed, all about him. And he was enjoying every minute of it. But then again, so was I.

I have to admit that when I first got the invitation to the preschool ball, my head flooded with all the things I should be doing instead of going. Thursday nights are always tough nights around our house due to the fact that the three older kids all have tests the next day. I thought of many little reasons why I should not go. But then I couldn't help but see the only reason I should go, and that was staring at me in the form of a very excited preschooler.

Walking into the social hall of the church where my son goes to preschool, I was amazed at how much trouble had gone into this event. A cardboard castle turned into a beanbag toss was in one corner. A makeshift garden of plastic flowers was in another. And you can't have a king and queen ball without crowns. Luckily, each child had made these that day at pre-school.

After a short while of game playing, the music started. Each preschooler lined up with their parental dates to await the rehearsed dance numbers.

The first song on the agenda was the ever-classic Chicken Dance. When the giggles over that one subsided, the Hokey-Pokey began.

What Parents Know by Heart

Then came the slow dance portion of the night. My little boy stretched out his little arms to hold my hands as we swayed to the music. Now, my youngest is not an overly affectionate child in most ways. In the last three years, he has not allowed anyone to kiss him without the kiss being wiped off. One time I mentioned to him that I kiss him when he's asleep. That night, he slept with all his covers over his head.

So when I can be swaying to the music, holding hands with this little anti-kissing bandit, the moment is all the more sweet. My little guy was looking at me with eyes that were dancing even more than his feet. And my own heart was keeping beat with the music.

Looking around the room at the other moms and dads dancing

with their little ones, I knew I was not the only one having such feelings.

I heard one dad upon leaving sum it up for all of us when he told the director of the preschool, "Thanks for this memory." And when it was time to go, my kingly escort, still holding my hand, sadly said, "Is it really over already? It went so fast." Somehow I suspect that will be my exact thought when these childhood years are also just a memory.

The
Book
of
Mom

IT'S A GIRL

"It's a girl."

Never have three words changed my life in such a dramatic way as those words did so many years ago.

I was thinking about the impact that declaration had on my life as I sat last week in the waiting room of Good Samaritan Hospital while my brother-in-law and sister-in-law waited in the labor and delivery room for their first child to arrive.

The timing was particularly poignant due to the fact that it was one day shy of being exactly fourteen years from the day that I, myself, was in the delivery room. It has been fourteen years since I was waiting for my firstborn to enter my life, changing it in a way I could never have imagined.

"It's a girl."

Indeed, the birth of all my children affected and changed me greatly, but nothing compares to that incredible shift in the axis of your world when you go from being a couple to being a family. And due to the fact that babies come only when they are good and ready, I had ample time in the waiting room to think about the affects of that time.

And since I am never one to wait to give advice until I am asked, I began to wonder what I could tell the parents-to-be about how this person they have waited to meet for nine months will change forever the way they think, sleep, act and even breathe.

But what could I say?

How could I explain to them that when you first hold that baby that weighs under ten pounds, you realize the weight of the world now rests in your arms?

What Parents Know by Heart

151

How can I tell them that when you first lay eyes on your child, you are not counting fingers and toes, but you are counting indescribable blessings?

How can you explain that thing your heart does when it feels like it will absolutely burst out of the confines of your chest?

And how can you explain to any parents-to-be that the next few days will be filled with tears? Tears of joy, tears of frustration, and sometimes tears for reasons only a parent's heart can understand.

And how can you possibly warn someone about that moment when you first leave the hospital and you realize that your beautiful baby—this precious present—is now one hundred percent dependent on you and you alone? Everything as you knew it, is changed. The other cars on the road now go too fast. When you walk toward your front door, holding your baby in your arms, you actually watch where you plant each foot before stepping.

Once you get inside the place where you live—the very place you just left a couple of days ago—you realize it, too, has changed. And with tears in your eyes, you manage to say, "Welcome home," as you realize the word "home" has never meant more to you in your entire life.

And how can you explain that from that moment on, you blink and a year—two years—ten—fourteen—have flown by?

How can I possibly explain all that and so much more to my brother-in-law and sister-in-law?

I guess I really don't have to.

They will find out soon enough by those same life-altering words.

It's a girl.

CHAPTER TEN:
The Loving Heart

*Just as I have loved you, you also should
love one another.*
—John 13:34

THE HAMMOCK

"Mommy, do you like butter?"

The question was not so much a taste survey for me as it was a trip down memory lane.

You see, the asker of the question was my youngest son who was cuddled up next to me in our backyard hammock. He was, of course, holding a freshly picked dandelion in his little hand as he held the lawn flower up to my chin to see if it would turn yellow indicating my butter bias.

"Yep," he matter-of-factly stated as he concluded his scientific experiment. "You like butter."

There is something about the hammock in my yard that makes me yearn for the simple things in life, like the dandelion butter test. For there is something about my hammock that beckons me to come and do that which I don't do very often: absolutely nothing.

And as I do absolutely nothing with my little guy next to me in the hammock, I feel an unspoken and yet definite connection to parents from generations before. Softly swaying in the breeze as we watch the birds land on the neighboring trees, I recognize that this is something parents and grandparents were doing years before I even came into the world. You can't get that same incredible connected feeling when you play a computer game with your child. While that can, admittedly, be enjoyable in its own right, I find myself playing those games and marveling at how fast things are changing. I always end up amazed and somewhat frightened at the pace of the world spinning around me.

But in my hammock, as we casually decide a simple fluffy cloud is actually a giant ice cream cone, I am reminded how beautifully basic things in life really are.

For in my hammock, my son and I spy a butterfly in the sky which promptly leads to tickling each others' cheeks by batting eyelashes to make butterfly kisses. Only after the butterfly kisses are completed do we move on to tickling each other's bare feet with our toes. Because in a hammock you just have to be barefoot.

So in my hammock, our feet have no more confinements than our imaginations. And as my son and I begin to tell stories about magical birds that talk and beautiful flowers that turn into elevators lifting you up to other mystical places, our imaginations soar.

I have to admit that in the course of most days, I feel lucky if I have had a chance to look into my children's eyes for more than a minute, let alone have a conversation with them. My family is as guilty as anyone else of getting so caught up in our schedules doing what the world tells us is important, that we sometimes forget what really is important.

So the preciousness of the moment when I can actually feel my child's heart beating in rhythm next to mine is not lost on me. Inside my house there most likely waits a towering pile of laundry. Directly around me there may be grass that needs cutting and flowers that need planting. And, of course, there's that dandelion problem to look into.

But right here in my hammock as my son and I continue to gently sway on this beautiful spring day, I have no more pressing thoughts on my mind than the deep desire to find a way to bottle the giggle of a child.

And, of course, to see if he likes butter.

155

What

Parents

Know

by

Heart

NOTES FROM HOME

It was late.

This is nothing unusual for me. Midnight tends to sneak up on me because bedtime at my house tends to get later every night. By the time school, sport and church activities are done for the day, the day is often done. Then, of course, there is homework. The last "goodnight" that I say to one of my kids is beginning to stretch beyond the time even I like to be awake.

But even when these "goodnights" are finished, my evening chores have just begun. There is more laundry to do, notes to read and sign, and clothes to lay out for the next school day. Then there are school lunches.

Nothing against the cafeteria selections at my kids' schools, but for some reason this year each of my kids wants to bring their lunch to school. Every day. For four days a week that means I am packing three lunches a night. And one night a week, I pack four.

This means that after all are finally in bed, I finally begin my assembly line production of peanut butter and jelly sandwiches accompanied by various side selections.

And once that chore is done, comes the longest portion of the night. I have no one to blame for this but myself.

You see, when my oldest started school, because I was a first time parent I felt the need to remain a part of her every waking moment even though she would be away from me, sitting at school for six hours a day. Accompanied by my over zealousness to encourage her newly developing reading skills, I began writing her little notes on the napkins that I put in her lunch box. The notes would sometimes rhyme, sometimes wish her good luck on a test and, oftentimes, just remind her I was thinking about her.

She seemed to enjoy this, so I kept doing it.

Then my second daughter started school. And I wrote her napkin notes. Then, my son began elementary school. And I wrote him napkin notes. And one day a week, my youngest eats lunch at preschool. And I'll bet you know what that means.

So my nighttime routine is getting longer by the minute. Once the lunches are packed, I then have to find a pen with which to compose these lunchtime letters. Now at my house, this is no small feat. I am hard-pressed to decide whether matching socks or pens disappear faster here. It's a close call.

And so it is that after scrounging around for a pen, I sit down with my unique stationery, and begin to compose.

Over the years this has not changed much—except for the fact that I now must sign my teenager's note "ILY, M" instead of the more embarrassingly affectionate "I love you, Mommy."

But the other night it was getting late. I had just packed the lunches and couldn't find one precious pen in the whole house. I decided it could wait. Tomorrow's napkins would have nothing more on them than the manufacturer had manufactured.

Then I went upstairs. As I was putting something away in my seven-year-old's room, I noticed his treasure box. This is where he keeps his important items like rocks and Pokemon cards. But I could see something else sticking up through these items. Inside his treasure box were many crumpled and worn napkins—with my little notes being saved forever alongside that which he treasured most.

I headed back downstairs with a lump in my throat. I would

find a pen if it was the last thing I'd do. And I will write those napkin notes as long as my kids will read them. I know they won't be reading mom's notes from home forever.

The day will come when my napkins with my silly scribbles will be thought of as simply a means to wipe their mouth after eating. But for now, I will treasure the position of importance while I can.

Before it's really too late.

AMAZING KIDS

"Please give this your utmost attention and return."

Thus began another year of back-to-school forms. And this year, with all four kids in the school system now, I was somewhat overwhelmed when I began to fill out one duplicated enrollment card after another.

Name. Address. Phone Number.

The more I filled out the vital information for my children, the more I realized how I wished I could tell the schools what really was vital about each of my kids. Yes, emergency medical forms serve a purpose, but our kids are so much more than the sum total of their allergies.

So when I am done filling in emergency phone numbers, I want to tell my five-year-old's kindergarten teacher something really important about my son. I want to tell her that he is more than ready to go to school this year. As the youngest child, he has done nothing but watch the others go and do and live. It is his turn now and he is thrilled. But his shyness might make you think he's not ready. Please don't give up on him. He's an amazing kid.

And after I have filled out all parental release forms, I want to tell my eight-year-old's teacher about him. I want to tell her that his heart is beautiful. And I know this for a fact because he wears it on his sleeve so often. And this breaks my heart because I know that school kids as well as society in general aren't always kind to little boys who live by their feelings. Please look out for him. He's an amazing kid.

And once I have written down what my children are to do in the event the school should ever close early, I want to tell my eleven-year-old daughter's teachers about her. I want to tell them about my daughter's dramatic flair. I want to tell them about her great sense of humor and how she loves to make people laugh. As a matter of fact, my daughter would do anything to make a friend happy. And as she dives into adolescence, that absolutely terrifies her mother. Please keep an eye on her. She's an amazing kid.

And upon completing the student directory form, I want to tell my fourteen-year-old daughter's teachers a few things. I want to tell them that going off to high school this year was hard, even for my most confident child. I want to tell her teachers that she will most likely never let them know she was nervous at all. No, she will most likely be as easy-going as always. It's just her nature. She will always smile. Please smile back at her. She's an amazing kid.

I guess when the very last form is filled out and filed away, and our children have filed into class for another year, we parents have one basic request we would make of their teachers. We are turning over to you our children. May you not just see them as a part of your classroom. But may you understand they are a part of our hearts.

Please give them your utmost attention. And return.

They are amazing kids.

SUNFLOWERS

"Why is mine the only one not growing?"

That lament is typical of youngest children everywhere. And so it was that it came from the five-year-old mouth of my youngest child.

We had recently planted a bunch of sunflower seeds. Everyone had his or her own flowerpots to tend. Moments after planting his seed, my youngest watched and waited for the new life to spring forth.

I tried explaining about how you have to wait for these things, they don't just happen overnight. But still, every morning my son would rush outside to take inventory on his watched pot. One by one he reported on the progress of the plants. One by one the little seeds sprouted stems that reached above the soil. One by one, my son noticed his pot was the only one not yet growing.

But that seemed so appropriate.

At five, my youngest is at the stage where he is painfully aware of everything that he can't do that others can do so well. "I'll race you to the swing set," he hopefully challenges his eight-year-old brother. Of course, eight-year-old legs naturally run faster than five-year-old legs. And the only thing more upsetting to a five-year-old than losing is harboring the suspicion that you simply let him win.

I watch his little face—his entire body—as he valiantly tries to keep up with his older brother and his brother's older friends. Always a step behind, but never really out of step, he makes up in determination what he might currently lack in skill. Still, I hear his need to push himself further.

What
Parents
Know
by
Heart

"I need to learn how to tie my shoes."

"I need to learn how to ride a bike."

"Why can't I hit the baseball every time?"

A year ago, after watching too much commercial television, he ran up to me and urgently announced, "Mommy, you need to buy me Hooked on Phonics because I'm in preschool and I can't read yet."

And so it was very characteristic of him that he impatiently waited for his sunflower to grow and bloom.

And as he watched and waited for what would develop, I couldn't help but think about what I was watching develop in my children. I guess watching kids grow is a little like watching a seed. When the seed is first in the ground, we have a vague idea of what it will be like when it fully blooms. But when it will fully bloom and what it will fully be, we never know until it is the exact time for us to know. We are anxious to see the final product, but we know better than to dig up the seed in order to check on the development. Instead, we patiently water it and give it light. And we wait. We know that eventually storms will come, but we pray that the roots will be strong enough to survive.

And like my five-year-old and his seed, there are days when I don't think I can detect any change at all in the growth of my children. But then there are days when I am absolutely astounded by the incredible change that has seemingly taken place over night.

This was the case with my youngest and his flowerpot. One highly anticipated day the seed of my youngest eventually sprouted. He now has the privilege of having the biggest and strongest sprout in the whole family. I am sure the flower that comes from it will be a source of great pride for him as it grows and reaches to the sun.

Already my five-year-old can barely contain his excitement as he declares, "Look how big it is getting! Isn't it amazing? And all this from a little seed!"

And I smile as I watch his eyes sparkle with the excitement of his accomplishment.

He took the words right out of my mouth.

163

What

Parents

Know

by

Heart